BAKER STUDIES IN BIBLI

The Philistines and the Old Testament

BAKER STUDIES IN BIBLICAL ARCHAEOLOGY

THE PHILISTINES AND THE OLD TESTAMENT

by Edward E. Hindson

BAKER BOOK HOUSE
Grand Rapids, Michigan 49506

ISBN: 0-8010-4034-5
Library of Congress Card Catalog Number: 72-182084

First printing, January 1972
Second printing, October 1975
Third printing, November 1977
Fourth printing, April 1980
Fifth printing, September 1981
Sixth printing, August 1983
Seventh printing, January 1986

We have received permission from the following authors/publishers to use their copyrighted illustrations:

41, 66, 70, 83	Kenyon, K. *Archaeology in the Holy Land.* New York: Praeger, 1966
43, 44	Garstang, J. *Joshua–Judges.* London: Constable & Co. 1931
52, 55	Dothan, M. and Freedman, D.N. *Ashdod I* (Atiqot, English Series VIII). Jerusalem: Israel Department of Antiquities and Museums, 1967 (pages 15 and 121 respectively)
62, 155	*Illustrated Family Encyclopedia of the Living Bible.* Chicago: San Francisco Productions, 1967
64	Winton, Thomas. *Archaeology and Old Testament Study.*
65	*Biblical Archaeologist* XXII (1959). Cambridge: American Schools of Oriental Research
68, 90	*Palestine Exploration Fund Annual.* London: 1912-13
74	Davidson, F. (ed) *The New Bible Dictionary.* Grand Rapids: Eerdmans, 1962
82	Albright, W.F. *Archaeology of Palestine.* 1960
84, 86	*Palestine Department of Antiquities Quarterly,* (5) Jerusalem: 1935-36
89	(top) Ashmolean Museum (bottom) Palestine Archaeological Museum
91	The British Museum
104	Macalister, R.A.S. *The Philistines: Their History and Civilization.* London: British Academy 1913

PHOTOLITHOPRINTED BY CUSHING - MALLOY, INC.
ANN ARBOR, MICHIGAN, UNITED STATES OF AMERICA

To beloved Professor Charles Shaw, S.T.D., who first introduced me to the serious study of the Old Testament and Archaeology.

Contents

Illustrations

Preface

Among all the ancient nations that played a major part in the early history of Israel, none is more important than the Philistines. They were the greatest threat to the national stability of the young nation of any enemy Israel faced. The Philistines thought that their superior culture and military prowess gave them a distinct advantage over the Hebrews who had only Yahweh on their side. The history of Israel as it relates to contacts with the Philistines is an expression of God's constant vindication of His people over all odds.

Some of Israel's greatest men were necessarily raised up to confront the Philistine threat: Samson, Samuel, Saul, David. The purpose of this work is to demonstrate from history and archaeology the significant place the Philistines occupy in the early history of Israel. Insights from archaeological data are also used to clarify the details of many of the narratives involving the Philistines. Special attention has been given to the origin and history of these peoples and their religious practices.

Special acknowledgment is due Dr. John Davis of Grace Theological Seminary, who assisted the author with the preparation of the manuscript. Gratitude is also expressed to the writer's former instructors in Old Testament at various institutions: Gleason Archer, Ph.D; Kenneth Barker, Th.M.; Herbert Bess, Ph.D.; Norman Geisler, M.A.; Walter Kaiser, M.A.; Charles Shaw, S.T.D.; John Whitcomb, Th.D.; G. Douglas Young, Ph.D. Their influence and instruction have been an invaluable incentive in the study of God's Word.

The author also wishes to thank the University of Michigan for the generous use of its graduate library. Finally a word of appreciation is due my wife, Donna, whose love and devotion have made this effort possible.

Edward E. Hindson
St. Petersburg
October, 1970

I

Historical Background

In the Old Testament the ancient "Sea People" are designated as the "Philistines" (*pelištîm*). who inhabited the area known as the "land of the Philistines" (*'pres pelistim*). Josephus calls them *allophuloi* and the Septuagint refers to them as *Phulistieim.*[1] The "land of the Philistines" also became known as "Philistia" (*pelešet*). Mitchell says that it is from these terms that the modern name "Palestine" is derived. He also states that this term is to be identified with the Egyptian *prst* and the Assyrian *palastu.*[2]

Not long after the Hebrew tribes came the Philistines moved into the world of the Canaanites and settled along the coastal plain between Jaffa and the desert region some fifty miles south of Gaza. Their eastern boundary became the junction between the alluvial coastal plain and the limestone plateau (Shephelah), which formed a buffer zone to the hill country of Judah.[3] It was along the coast that they became

---

[1] See the thorough discussion in R. A. S. Macalister, *The Philistines: Their History and Civilization* (London: British Academy, 1911), pp. 1-2.

[2] T. C. Mitchell, "Philistines," J. Douglas (ed.), *The New Bible Dictionary* (Grand Rapids: Eerdmans, 1962), p. 988.

[3] D. Baly, *Geography of the Bible* (New York: Harper and Row, 1957) pp. 138-47.

the ruling class in five old Canaanite city kingdoms, and called them Gaza, Ashdod, Askelon, Ekron, and Gath.[4] They also began to push inland and had a strong influence in Joppa, Jabneel, Gerar, and Sharuhen.[5] Only Ashkelon was located on the sea coast. The others were cut off by coastal sand dunes. Ashdod, for example, used Ashdod-yam, which was two and a half miles away, as a port.[6]

That other "Sea Peoples" settled to the north is known from the letter of the Egyptian official Wen-Amun.[7] In about 1000 B.C. he stated that *Tkr* were living in the city of Dor, south of Mount Carmel. Alt says that other "Sea Peoples" related to the Philistines may have advanced into the Plain of Jezreel and settled there near Beth-shan.[8] At Beth-shan pottery coffins have been discovered containing corpses with gold mouthplates. This is an Aegean burial practice[9] and poses the question regarding the origin of these "Sea Peoples."

Origin of the "Philistines"

The Scripture tells us that the Philistines "came out from" Caphtor (*Casluhim*). They were sons of Mizraim (Egypt) and of Ham.[10] Most historians agree that they came from the eastern Mediterranean area but their original homeland and

---

[4] See M. Noth, *The Old Testament World* (Philadelphia: Fortress Press, 1966), p. 78.

[5] This is discussed by T. C. Mitchell, "Philistia," in D. W. Thomas (ed.), *Archaeology and the Old Testament Study* (Oxford: Clarendon Press, 1967), p. 405.

[6] *Ibid.,* p. 406.

[7] J. Pritchard, *Ancient Near Eastern Texts* (Princeton: Princeton University Press, 1950), pp. 25-29.

[8] Cf., A. Alt, *Palästinajahrbuch,* xxii, pp. 118-19; and note the historical role of Beth-shan in Saul's final battle with the Philistines (I Sam. 31).

[9] Cf., J. Gray, *Archaeology and the Old Testament World* (New York: Harper & Row, 1962), p. 126.

[10] Cf., I Chron. 1:12 and Amos 9:7.

migration route are uncertain.[11] It is quite probable that they stopped at Crete, called Caphtor in the Old Testament (Jer. 47:4; Amos 9:7). Also the term *kerethi* ("Cretans") is used in Ezek. 25:16; Zeph. 2:5; I Sam. 30:14, to designate the "Philistines."

Early Palestine was dominated by white Caucasians from the eastern Mediterranean area. At the end of the third millennium B.C. there is evidence for the influx of new peoples into Palestine. This is attested in the tombs at Tell el-'Ajjul.[12] The bearers of this culture were seafaring nomads who stopped at Cyprus, providing an indirect contact with the Aegean area. The Middle Bronze Age gives both archaeological and textual evidence of extensive trade between Syria, Egypt, and Crete.[13] Gardiner says it is probable that the names *kftyw* in Egyptian documents and the Babylonian term *kaptara* in this period are to be connected with the Biblical Caphtor, and are to be identified with some part of the Aegean area, probably Crete.[14]

These "Sea Peoples" collectively were the Luka, Sherden, Danuna, Adawasha, Tursha, Sheklesh, Weshesh, Peleset, and Tjekker.[15] Within two centuries they descended from the north and west upon the Levant coast. Mitchell feels they originated in the Aegean region and migrated to Anatolia and then eastward.[16]

The Philistines settled in Canaan during the time of the Israelite judges (twelfth to eleventh century B.C.) and threatened Israel inland. The five-city league formed the basis of their government, with each city ruled by a "lord" *(seren)*. A

---

[11] Cf., the comments of Noth, *op. cit.*, p. 78.

[12] Mitchell, *AOTS*, p. 406.

[13] *Ibid.*, p. 408.

[14] A. Gardiner, *Ancient Egyptian Onomastica*, 1947, p. 202 f., cf. also J. Pendlebury, *The Archaeology of Crete* (New York: Biblo & Tannen, 1963), pp. 47-59.

[15] Cf., list from Mitchell, *AOTS*, p. 410.

[16] *Ibid.*, p. 410.

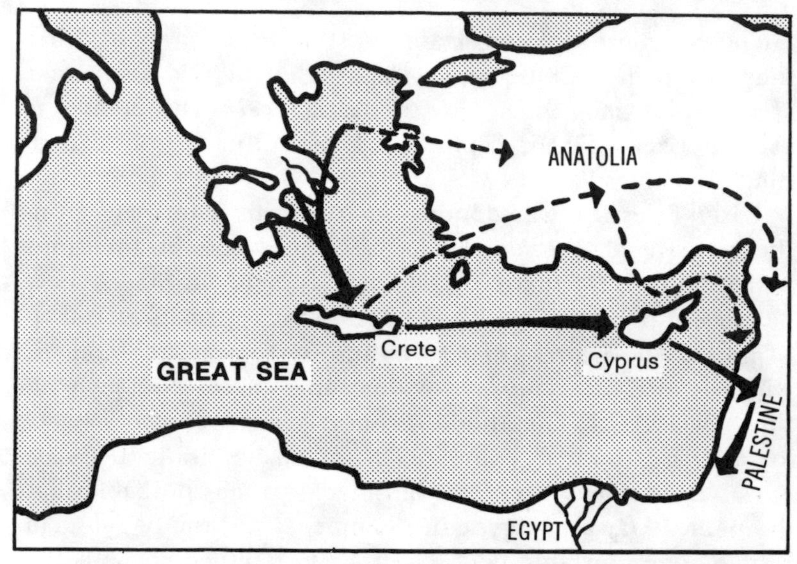

Migrations of the "Sea People"

central shrine to Dagon at Ashdod was the rallying point of the Philistine confederacy.[17]

One of the problems for Bible students has been the reference to "Philistines" before the time of the judges. In the book of Genesis we read of Abraham's contacts with them (21:32, 34) and their king, Abimelech of Gerar. Many critical writers have attempted to wipe this off as an anachronism, since the great influx of Philistines into Canaan was not until a much later period.[18] Others have suggested that a later copiest inserted the term "Philistine" to refer to a similar group of original coastal people.[19] It seems most

---

[17] J. Graybill, "Philistines," M. Tenney (ed.), *Zondervan Pictorial Bible Dictionary* (Grand Rapids: Zondervan, 1963), p. 651.

[18] Cf., an example in J. Bright, *A History of Israel,* pp. 73-74. Cf. on the arrival of Philistines in Canaan, E. Anati, *Palestine Before the Hebrews* (New York: Knopf, 1963), p. 11.

[19] Note that Mitchell hints at this in *AOTS,* pp. 408-09; but in *NBD,* p. 990, he takes a much stronger stand.

reasonable, however, in light of recent discoveries and the clear statement of the text to conclude that there really were small, early settlements of Philistines in the land in patriarchal times.

Albright feels that mule caravan trade was at its peak in the Near East at this time, and that Abraham was engaged in this trade.[20] He probably traded in the sector between Palestine and Egypt. Abraham is said to have lived in the "land of the Philistines" at this time, while Abimelech was king (Gen. 26:1, 14, 15). Since this same person is said to have had dealings with Isaac also, it is possible that *'abîmelek* ("my father is king") is a Semitic title adopted by Philistine rulers, rather than a personal name. Mitchell points out that a minority group of foreigners would likely accommodate in this way to gain the confidence of the people. Though Abi-melech is a Semitic name, Phicol (commander of the army) is probably non-Semitic.

During this time a great migration of Central Europeans was under way and it is likely that as they swept down into the Aegean area many of the "Sea Peoples" were forced eastward, eventually into the Hittite Empire and Palestine. In the meantime, Ramses III had to meet the Peleset and Tjekker in a new onslaught of "Sea Peoples."[21] There is evidence of a major expansion of Aegean trade in the Middle Minoan II period (c. 1900-1700 B.C.). Objects of Aegean origin and manufacture have been found at Ras Shamra, Hazor, Megiddo, Tod, Harageh, Lahun, and Abydos.[22] There is extensive evidence of early Aegean contacts with the Near East by the time the Mycenaean culture of mainland Greece replaced the old Minoan civilization of Crete. Bichrome ware from Cyprus and Cilicia is well attested in Palestine in the sixteenth

20 Albright, *BASOR*, 163, 1961, pp. 36-54.

21 Mitchell, *AOTS*, p. 412.

22 Mitchell, *NBD*, p. 990.

century B.C., and by the fifteenth century Ashdod and Ashkelon are mentioned as established trading centers in Ugaritic documents.[23] The Amarna Letters include correspondence from the ruler of Ashkelon and mention Gath, Gaza, and Joppa. They also reveal the use of Hurrian and Indo-European names (such as Widya).[24]

These evidences indicate established settlements which must themselves be the result of earlier migrations. The Haribu were already causing troublesome invasions by this time, assisted by Ashkelon. Pottery from these times shows a great similarity between Philistia and the Aegean peoples.[25] By the tenth century B.C. they disappeared along with Philistine power which David finally suppressed.[26]

During the period between the Exodus and the establishment of the Hebrew monarchy, the inscription of Ramses III (1168-1137) describes the invasion of the "Sea Peoples," including the Philistines, who were halted in a great "folk-movement" south along the Syrian coast. The invaders were allowed to occupy the Palestinian coast under the suzerainity of Egypt.[27] Ramses claimed: "I settled them in strongholds bound in my name."[28]

In the records of Ramses II, the account of the battle of Kadesh in the fourteenth century names the Lukku among those fighting with the Hittites and the Sherden with Egypt. Aegean contacts with the Near East continued in the thirteenth century as shown by late Helladic III B style pottery at 'Askalon, Tell el 'Hesi, Tell el-'Ajjul, Tell Gemmeh and Tell

---

[23] D. Freedman, *Biblical Archaeologist,* xxvi, 1963, p. 136.

[24] Cf., Albright, *Cambridge Ancient History,* ii, xx, p. 12 f.

[25] See the extensive comments of G. E. Wright, *Biblical Archaeologist,* 1957, pp. 94-96.

[26] Cf., comments of Albright, *Archaeology and the Religion of Israel,* (Baltimore: Johns Hopkins Press, 1953), p. 127.

[27] Cf., the discussion in Gray, *op. cit.,* p. 78.

[28] J. Breasted, *A History of Egypt,* iv, 62, 1906.

el-Far'ah.[29] Also a group of Cretan seals found near Gaza imply an Aegean colony there.[30] Ramses' successor, Merneptah had to again repel the invading "Sea Peoples." His inscription mentions Gezer and Ashkelon.

From the time of their settlement on the coast the Philistines began to push inland. The triumphal relief carvings which adorn the Ramses III temple at Medinet Habu shows battle scenes involving Peleset, Tjekker, and Sherden as Egyptian warriors, wearing a headdress similar to that worn in seventeenth to sixteenth century Crete, sixteenth century Mycenae, and thirteenth to twelfth century Cyprus. Also many Aegean-type weapons (ribbed corselets, round shields, long broad-swords and triangular daggers) have been found near Jaffa and even in the area of the Caucasus (south Russia).[31]

The end of the second millennium B.C. was the transition from the Bronze Age to the Iron Age. The Philistines may have learned the technology of iron-working in Anatolia for they gained an early monopoly in this skill in Palestine (cf., I Sam. 13:19-22). In the early part of this period (c. 1200-900 B.C.) distinctive pottery associated with sites in the coastal plain occupied by the Philistines are found as far inland as Jerusalem and Tell en-Nasbeh (Mizpah).[32] According to I Samuel 13, the Philistines were establishing garrisons within Saul's own territory.

A number of anthropoid clay coffins found at Beth-shan and Tell el-Far'ah, in association with Philistine pottery, are probably to be connected with the Philistines.[33] Mitchell

---

29 Cf., more extensive discussion in Mitchell, *AOTS,* p. 411.

30 Cf., detailed study by V. Kenna, *Cretan Seals,* 1960, p. 65, 78, 151 f.

31 Cf., discussion in R. Maxwell-Hyslop, *Iraq,* viii, 1946, pp. 47-60.

32 Gray, *op. cit.*, p. 126.

33 This has been the evaluation of many archaeologists and writers. Cf. comments of T. Dothan, "Archaeological Reflections on the Philistine Problem," *Antiquity and Survival,* ii, 1957, pp. 151-64; G. E. Wright, "Philistine Coffins and Mercenaries," *Biblical Archaeologist Reader II* (New York: Doubleday, 1964).

follows Wright in suggesting that they may have copied these practices from Egypt while being Egyptian mercenaries.[34] The widespread distribution of these remains illustrates the influence and spread of the Philistines.[35]

The story of Wen-Amun, the Egyptian traveler, shows that in the early eleventh century B.C. the Philistines' associate, the Tjekker, was engaged in profitable sea trade in Palestine, and the same is likely of the Philistines.[36]

All this evidence shows significant early traces of the Philistines in the Near East before the eleventh century, the time of their greatest power. It is quite possible, therefore, that such a strong settlement and penetration of these people would have been preceded by smaller and earlier attempts. Since there is little evidence of the Aegean peoples anywhere (as contrasted with the Near Eastern peoples) it is an argument only from silence, based on critical presuppositions, to deny any validity to the Genesis reference to "Philistines."[37] Kitchen presents a strong voice for accepting the narrative.[38] He refers to the mention of the Caphtorim in Deuteronomy 2:23 and to the reference to Kaptara (Caphtor) in the Mari tablets of the patriarchal era. He notes that one document even mentions a King of Hazor in Palestine sending gifts to Kaptara. He also observes that traffic in the reverse direction is substantiated by the occurrence of Middle Minoan II pot-

---

[34] Mitchell, *AOTS*, p. 414.

[35] For a detailed discussion of their distribution see, Albright, *Cambridge Ancient History*, ii, ch. xxxiii, p. 27.

[36] Cf., the complete story in J. Pritchard, *Ancient Near Eastern Texts*, pp. 25-29.

[37] This is the attitude and approach of J. Bright, *A History of Israel* (Philadelphia: Westminster, 1959), p. 73, where he regards this anachronism as a "modernizing touch" by a later redactor.

[38] Cf., his very fine discussions in his lucid and well-documented style. K. A. Kitchen, *Ancient Orient and Old Testament* (Chicago: Inter-Varsity Press, 1966), pp. 80-81.

tery at Hazor, Ugarit, and even in Upper Egypt.[39] Kaufmann of the Hebrew University also relates the ancient (patriarchal) Philistines to the Caphtorim settled in Gerar and Beer-sheba.[40]

One's final answer to the "problem" of the mention of Philistines in the patriarchal age will depend on his attitude and approach toward Scripture. If he believes its claim to be the Word of God he will attempt to "harmonize" any so-called discrepancies. If he takes a critical presuppositional framework, he will deny the possibility of the reference. The first attitude is the Scriptural one, and there is sufficient, though limited, evidence for the possibility of "Philistines" of Aegean origin in Palestine before the time of the judges.

PHILISTINE CONTACT WITH ISRAEL

This was one of the most formative eras in Israel's history.[41] By the time of the Hebrew conquest of Canaan the Philistines were so powerful that none of their towns were taken (cf., Judg. 3:3). By the time of Samson (c. 1150 B.C.) they appear as oppressors of Israel for forty years (Judg. 13:1; 15:20). In the last year of Eli (I Sam. 4:1) the Philistines attacked the hill country near Mizpah where they captured the ark. This was the Israelites' most severe defeat at that time. The Philistines destroyed the religious center at Shiloh (Khirbet Seilun) in the Samarian hill country[42] and controlled much of the Plain of Esdraelon, the Shephelah,

---

39 Note his detailed references to the discoveries of Dossin, Yadin, Malamat, Schaeffer; *ibid.*, p. 81.

40 Y. Kaufmann, *The Biblical Account of the Conquest of Palestine* (Jerusalem: Magnes Press, 1953), p. 50.

41 Cf., the fine discussion of this period in F. F. Bruce, *Israel and the Nations* (Grand Rapids: Eerdmans, 1963), pp. 21-27. He gives a very helpful survey of the relationship of the Philistine "invasion" to the establishment of the Hebrew monarchy.

42 For a note on the excavations at Shiloh, see M. Noth, *op. cit.*, p. 131.

the Negeb, and even parts of the Judean hills.[43] Eventually they were driven back to the coast by Samuel (I Sam. 7:12-14), Jonathan (I Sam. 14:1-47), and David (I Sam. 17; II Sam. 5:17).[44] By the time of Solomon all of Philistia was under subjection to Israel (I Kings 4:21).

Philistia had at the mid-eleventh century B.C. reached the peak of its greatest power and importance. Lying on one of the most convenient trade routes between Egypt and Syria, the nation held a key place in the Near East. From the early second millennium B.C. people living along this section of the coast were engaged in important sea trade. This is clearly indicated by pottery recovered from the sea, which shows a heavy concentration off Philistia with little else south of Carmel. Most of these discoveries have been opposite Ashkelon and Ashdod.[45] The Philistines were also prominent road builders. Their highways (*mesillah*) were used to connect to Israelite towns. The Philistine city of Ekron, for example, was linked to Beth-shemesh by a *messilah* (I Sam. 6:12).[46]

Even David used Philistine mercenaries in his bodyguard. In II Sam. 8:18 the phrase *k*^{e}*rētî u-p*^{ē}*lethî* means "Cretans and Philistines." Mitchell suggests that *p*^{e}*lētî* is probably an

---

[43] For evidence of Philistine penetration even into the Jordan Valley see C. Gordon, *Introduction to Old Testament Times* (Ventor, New Jersey: Ventor Publishers, 1953), p. 109 f. He discusses finds of Philistine pottery in Jordan Valley and also notes that "Jordan" is the Cretan word for "river" (*Iardonos*) and is used as a common noun meaning "river." Cf., Joshua 4:22–"this Jordan."

[44] It is not our purpose here to give a detailed discussion of this period of history. Such references will be made as related to the consideration of this Philistine religion. For a thorough Biblical history of the events between Israel and the Philistines the reader should examine the articles on "Philistines" in J. McClintock and J. Strong (ed.) *Cyclopedia of Biblical, Theological and Ecclesiastical Literature* (New York: Harper & Brothers, 1891 Reprint. Grand Rapids: Baker Book House, 1970.), Vol. VIII, pp. 102-08; J. Orr (ed.), *The International Standard Bible Encyclopedia* (Chicago: Howard-Severance, 1915), Vol. IV., pp. 2376-80. These discussions give more relevance to the Scriptural data than does Albright, *Archaeology and the Religion of Israel,* pp. 111-12. He denies any real historical basis for the Shamgar and Samson episodes.

[45] Cf., details in D. Barag, *Israel Exploration Journal,* xiii, 1963, pp. 13-19.

[46] Noth, *op. cit.,* p. 85.

analogical adaptation of the regular form, *pelištî*, to make it assonant with *kerētî*.[47] Other terms borrowed as "loan words" indicate the objects introduced into Palestine by the Philistines. "Helmet" (*kôbaʾ* and *ḳôba*) first appears in the account of Goliath's armor (I Sam. 17) and is probably cognate with the Hittite *kupaḫi* ("helmet, headdress").[48] The term *ʾargaz* ("box, chest") is used in the Old Testament to refer to the box in which the Philistines placed the gold images which they returned with the ark (I Sam. 6:8, 11, 15). It is possibly cognate with the Hittite *ark* ("to shut in") and the Greek *arkos* ("protection").[49]

Two Philistine names used with probable west Anatolian connections are Goliath and Achish. In *golyat* the element *-yat* may be cognate with *wattaš* found in the names of the western foes of the Hittites, while *ʾakîš* is found in a list of what are described as *kftiw* names on an Egyptian school tablet (eighteenth dynasty). It is probably cognate to Anchises, who according to Homer was a Trojan, father of Aeneas.[50]

That the Philistine influence in Israel was strong is quite clear. The Hebrews dwelt beside these people throughout their history. Even the system of double and crossed wall, with storage space between, was borrowed from the Philistines.[51] Such a study of the cultural origin and background of the Philistines casts much light on the study of their religious practices. In the area of military practice we see many parallels. The idea of battle by "championship" suggested to Israel by Goliath was of Aegean origin and implied that whichever had the stronger god would win the contest

47 Mitchell, *AOTS*, p. 424 n.

48 Cf., discussion in Sapir, *JAOS*, lvii, 1937, pp. 73-77. Also see the illustrations of these helmets in McClintock and Strong, *op. cit.*, viii pp. 102-08.

49 Mitchell, *AOTS*, p. 415.

50 *Ibid.*

51 Cf., Gray, *op. cit.*, p. 126.

and any further battle would be unnecessary for the winner would be obvious. This explains why the Philistines fled when Goliath fell.

II

Philistine Religion and Practices

RELIGIOUS INSTITUTIONS OF THE PHILISTINES

The religion of the Philistines is a very difficult matter to trace because little is known of it apart from brief references in the Old Testament.[1] Since their dcities (Dagon, Ashtoreth, and Baal-zebub) have Semitic names it is most obvious that the Philistines assumed much of the Canaanite religious concepts when they arrived in Palestine. It is unlikely, however, that they merely adopted the complete religious system they found there. Rather, they probably brought a strong religious heritage with them and accommodated some of the Semitic names, terminology and practices, so as to be acceptable with the Canaanite peoples.[2]

Ashtoreth had a temple at Beth-shan where the Canaanite deity Ashtoreth was already well-established in pre-Philistine

---

[1] Cf., Macalister, *op. cit.,* pp. 90-114 for an attempted "reconstruction" based on very late evidence from the temple at Gaza in the Hellenistic era. It is very uncertain that this situation may be used to explain what the early Philistine worship involved. Since the Philistines seem to have been "culture vultures" it is unlikely that a temple in the Christian era would still adhere to Philistine practices of a millennium before. The author would have done better to give more prominence to the Biblical accounts.

[2] Mitchell, *AOTS,* p. 415, says that by the time of the Philistine struggle with Israel much of their culture had been accommodated to that of the Canaanites.

times.[3] It was here that the trophies of Saul and his family were hung from the wall.

There was a temple of Dagon at Ashdod. He was the universal deity of the Philistines who, unlike the Semites, were not limited to localized deities (i.e., Baʾalim). The sculptured image of the god stood in the temple where the priests had the rite of "leaping on the threshhold" rather than stepping over it.[4] Dagon also had a temple at Gaza where Samson was taken after his capture and humiliation. This was a large structure which differed drastically from the native "high places" of Palestine. According to Judges 16:23, temple sacrifices were offered at Gaza by the "lords" of the Philistines. Macalister suggests that they probably intended to offer Samson at their annual festival.[5]

It appears that the Philistine religion had little influence upon the Hebrews for it is given only a brief and rare reference in Judges 10:6. It is likely that in spite of the Semitization of the Philistines, their cult remained too exotic to attract the Semitic temperament. If the Place of the Four Ways in the Christian era was still an accurate reflection of Philistine practices we may obtain some idea of their cultus.[6] There was a large marble pillar of Aphrodite above a stone altar and women came to burn incense and light lamps to her. She was supposed to give dreams and advice to those seeking matrimony.[7] This was all carried out in an exotic and mysterious manner.

The five prominent towns had organized a confederacy under the Anakim as early as the time of Joshua and were

---

[3] Cf., A. Rowe, *The Four Canaanite Temples of Beth-shan,* part i, 1940, pp. 31-34.

[4] Cf., the extensive discussion in Macalister, *op. cit.,* p. 90-91.

[5] *Ibid.* He is reminded of the Athenian *Thargēlia* with Samson in the role of the *pharmakos.* He notes that human sacrifices were still practiced at the temple of Marna at Gaza in the fourth century A.D.

[6] Macalister, *Ibid.,* pp. 108-09, seems to accept this as valid evidence.

[7] *Ibid.* It is interesting to note the parallel to many Roman Catholic practices.

bound together in an amphictyonic state. They were evidently not a numerous people but rather an Aegean military aristocracy ruling a predominantly Canaanite population.[8] It has been suggested that the political authority was exercised by Gaza in an hegemony over the others, for in the lists of the towns it is mentioned first (Josh. 13:3; Amos 1:7-8). Ashdod (I Sam. 6:17) seems to have been the religious center of the "nation." Ekron always stands last in the lists while Ashdod, Ashkelon, and Gath interchange places.[9] Each town possessed its own territory, including dependent towns, or "daughters" (cf. Josh. 15:45-47; I Chron. 18:1; II Sam. 1:20; Ezek. 16:27, 57). These factors explain why these people could easily amalgamate themselves and their religion with the people whom they ruled.

DEITIES OF THE PHILISTINES

1. Baal-zebub

This deity was widely known in Palestine (note reference in New Testament in Matt. 12:24, to "Prince of Devils"). When the Philistines captured Ekron, the local deity, the Semitic Baal-zebub had already become "Lord of the Flies." This was no derogatory phrase for in the summer and autumn this area swarms with all sorts of flies, gnats, mosquitoes, and other winged pests of the Shephelah. Since Baal-zebub is associated with the giving of oracles, it is probable that he was thought to give oracles by his flies.[10] A hint in Isaiah 2:6 shows that the Philistines, like the Etruscans, were skilled in soothsaying and it is likely that more Philistines than just Amaziah went to their oracles. "Baal-Prince" is read from Baal-zebul attested in Ugaritic as *zbl.b'l.*

---

[8] Cf., the thorough discussion in Bright, *op. cit.,* pp. 164-174.

[9] Cf., McClintock and Strong, *op. cit.,* p. 107.

[10] Cf., statements by Macalister, *op. cit.,* p. 92.

2. Ashtoreth

This god represents a partial assimilation by the Philistines of the deity of the land they conquered, for Ashtoreth was the chief feminine Semitic deity. There was a real distinction between this deity and Aphrodite, though they were similar and often confused. This is borne out by the inscription of Damon of Ashkelon who addresses his tutelary deities, saying:

DII OURIŌI KAI ASTARTHI PALASTIĒI
KAI APHRODITĒI OURANIAI THEOIS EPĒKOOIS
DAMŌN DĒMĒTRIOU ASKAAŌEITĒS
SŌTHEIS APO PEIRATŌN
EUCHĒ
OG THEMITON DE PROSATEIĒ
AIGEIOĒ UIKON BOOS THĒLEIAS[11]

Herodotus (i. 105) notes the temple of *ē Ourania Aphroditē* standing at Ashkelon. The goddess of Phonecia was called Derketo, a Greek corruption of the Semitic Atargatis. *ʿAtr* is a variation of Ashtart, depicted as a fishman. Sacred fish were kept at her temple and at one time the Syrians would not even eat fish.[12]

The Philistine element in the Ashkelonite Atargatis is almost identical to the legend told in Crete in Callimachus' "Hymn to Artemis," in which Britomartis was beloved of Artemis and was chased by Monos. She leaped into the sea to escape and a fish net saved her. Old legends distinctly tell of a Syrian goddess actually dedicated to a deity who fled from an unknown lover and who was directly connected with Crete.[13]

---

11 *Ibid.*, p. 94.

12 *Ibid.*, p. 96.

13 Cf., *ibid.*, pp. 97-98. Watch out for his attitude toward Jonah as an allegory parallel to the Cretan-Carian legends of sea-monsters near Joppa.

It is possible that the cult of Britomartis was brought from the Aegean region by the Philistines who arrived in Palestine and told the same tales of Ashtoreth as they had known of Britomartis.[14] They built temples to her (a thing unheard of in Canaan before). These sea coast peoples transferred their tales of sea creatures, sea monsters, mermaids, and sacred fish to their new surroundings.

3. Dagon

The head of the Philistine pantheon of deities was Dagon who had temples at Gaza, Ashdod, Beth-shan.[15] The temple at Gaza is referred to in the Samson incident. The temple at Ashdod had a large image of Dagon (something unknown in the crude Canaanite shrines). Josephus called it a *xoanon,* indicating that it was probably made of wood. It is mentioned in I Samuel 5:1-5 as the place where the Israelites' captured ark was taken and kept two nights. This passage includes a reference to the "priests of Dagon" and is the only reference to Philistine priests. While the ark remained in the temple of Dagon the first night the image fell on its face before it and the second night it fell and its head and hands were broken off, so that "only (the stump of) Dagon remained." This is difficult to translate, for "stump of" has been supplied to clarify the text. Macalister mentions Wellhausen's dropping the *n* from *dāgon* to read "only his fish was left."[16] Though he too accepts the theory that Dagon was half-fish—half-man, he notes that the Greek text represents a fuller text: *kai kephalē Dagōn [dai amphotepa ta ichnē cheirōn autou aphērēmena epi ta emprosthia amapheth*

[14] Cf., comments of Condor, "Philistines," *International Standard Bible Encyclopedia* Vol. 4 (Chicago: Howard-Severance, 1915), p. 2377. He connects Ashtoreth with the Akkadian Istar.

[15] Jerome in commenting on Isaiah 46:1 refers to still other temples as well: "siue, iuxta LXX, Dagon, qui tamen in Hebraico non habetur. Et est idolum Ascalonis, Gazae, et reliquarum urbium Philisthiim."

[16] Macalister, *op. cit.,* p. 101.

ekastoi] kai amphorterai oi karpoi tōn cheirōn autou peptōkotes epi to prothupon, plēn ē rachis Dagōn upeleiphthē.[17] The bracketed words do not appear in the Hebrew text. This translation, however, mentions the "feet" which would go against the fish view if the bottom half were the fish part. The term "backbone" is really a technical term for the "pedestal" on which the image stood. Therefore it is debatable whether the text should read: "only the fish-half remained" or "only the pedestal remained," although according to recent archaeological discoveries, the latter is more likely.

"Dagon" was a Semitic name derived either from *dāg*, "fish" or *dāgān*, "grain." There is clear evidence of Dagon in Palestine before the Philistines ever came. Dagon-takalam is mentioned in two letters from Tell el-Amarna, while the name Beth-Dagon appears in several Palestinian villages and in the list of Asiatic towns conquered by Ramses III at Medinet Habu.[18] The name "Dagon" also appears in Mesopotamia in cuneiform signs to be read Da-gān (third millennium B.C.). At Babylon there was a king named Idin-Dagān and his son Isme-Dagān. Also a seal-cylinder of Dagān-bilu-uṣur (c. 850 B.C.) has been attested along with several references to Dagan and Anu in the cosmogonies. After the ninth century the name disappears.[19]

Macalister, who is the only writer on the Philistines who attempts to give any extensive comments on their religion, accepts Dagon and Dagān as the same being with a conflation between them similar to the one he sees between Britomartis and Atargatis.[20] He notes that the Etruscans, who were akin to the Philistines, had a myth about Tages, who appeared as a

---

[17] *Ibid.*

[18] *Bty-Dkn* is Beth-Dagon in Egyptian.

[19] For detailed notes and comments on Dag-an see Macalister, *op. cit.*, p. 104. Cf., also Išmē-Dagon, son of Šamši-Adad in the Mari letters.

[20] *Ibid.*, p. 105.

boy to teach the people soothsaying. Since the Etruscans rejected the letter "D," Tag would be comparable to Dag. Macalister submits that the Philistines possibly identified their Dages with the Canaanite Dagon who was known in the Near East from the third millennium as the deity of the weather or fertility rites.[21] It is quite possible that the Philistines who borrowed the clay writing tablet, burial ideas, and many other customs from the Near East could also have "borrowed" their god by assimilating him into their religious heritage.

Recent archaeological discoveries have made it virtually certain that Dagon is to be associated with a "grain deity" or fertility god.[22] In Ugarit he was considered the father of Baal who is definitely connected with the agrarian culture and fertility cult of the Canaanites. Dagon was commonly worshiped in Mesopotamia in the third millennium B.C. and was brought to the eastern-Mediterranean countries by the Semitic migrations of the second millennium B.C.

RELIGIOUS PRACTICES OF THE PHILISTINES

The Philistines appear to have been deeply imbued with superstition, for they carried their idols with them on their battle campaigns (II Sam. 5:21). These small, portable images (*ʿaṣᵉbîm*) were carried as good luck amulets. News of their victories was proclaimed before them and the crowds at the image-houses (I Sam. 31:9). In II Macc. 12:40 we are told that later Philistines also carried charms that had been presented before idols. These warrior-minded peoples were very concerned about the gods' favor upon them in battle.

Also attached to the Philistine seats of worship were

21 Cf., Mitchell, *AOTS*, p. 415.

22 Cf., J. Davis, *Conquest and Crisis* (Grand Rapids: Baker, 1969), p. 140. He notes that the derivation of the deity's name is *dāgān*, the Hebrew word for "grain."

priests and diviners (I Sam. 6:2). Philistine magicians were highly esteemed (cf., Isa. 2:6). Even Hebrew King Amaziah consulted the oracle of Baal-zebub (II Kings 1:2). The fact that all the Philistines recognized the same gods indicates that they recognized the extra-territorial jurisdiction of their deities and others also. For example, they feared the power of Yahweh in the incident involving the ark at Ashdod and sent presents to Him as the ark was returned to the Israelites.[23] This action indicates that the polytheistic Philistines believed Yahweh to be real and to have power even in their territory, whereas the Canaanites believed that a god had power only within his own confined locale.

This attitude is also an indication of the Aegean origin of the concept of the powers of the gods in battle. The nation whose gods were the strongest, cleverest, and most willing to help was always the victor. The Canaanites followed a similar contest but Canaanite gods lacked the personality, cleverness, and stubborness of the many deities of the Aegean peoples. Following this belief the Philistines adopted a procedure clearly taken from their ancestors: victory by championship battle. Of course the clearest indication of this is in the David and Goliath episode. Such a practice of one man representing an entire army was unheard of among the Semitic peoples who believed in the corporate unity of the nation in battle.[24] This will explain several so-called "problems" in the narrative of I Samuel 17.

First, consider why no one gave even the slightest response

---

[23] M. Woudstra, *The Ark of the Covenant from Conquest to Kingship* (Philadelphia: Presbyterian & Reformed, 1965), pp. 30-34; 103-126, for a discussion of the relationship between the ark and the presence of God.

[24] Cf., H. W. Robinson, *Corporate Personality in Ancient Israel* (Philadelphia: Fortress Press, 1964); he notes that the action of an individual could often affect the entire nation of Israel (i.e. Achan, Jacob, Rachel). But only in this sense did the Hebrews know of any "representatives." Battle by championship was not regularly followed among the Israelites, for they were God's nation and He used the whole nation to accomplish his purposes.

to the challenge. It is true that they were afraid of Goliath's prowess but is it not possible that they were totally unaccustomed to such a procedure? Also, remember that he challenged Israel day and night for forty days (v. 16). In the meanwhile Saul was seeking a man to fight for Israel and promised him a great reward (v. 25). The content of the challenge was to let each side send out its champion to battle each other. Whoever won the championship battle would secure victory for his nation. It is clear that such a concept was based on the power of the gods. If the gods of the Philistines could give the champion victory then they could surely give the nation victory. Therefore, the test of such a battle was a test of the power of the gods. This explains why Goliath made such a mockery of the God of the Israelites (v. 45). If He could not empower their champion, then He could not give victory to their nation.

It has always been questioned that Saul allowed a youth, despite his oral confession of faith in Yahweh, to represent all Israel in this battle. It should be noted that up to this point the battle was at a standstill.[25] Not only was Israel unable to win but also the Philistine army was unable to gain the victory. Saul was not always a man of his word and it is quite likely that though he hoped David would win, he never intended to give up to the Philistine army if David did not defeat Goliath. Notice the final result. When Goliath fell and the Philistines saw that he was dead, they fled. Why? Because they recognized the validity of the concept of battle by championship. They believed that Yahweh had beaten their gods and they ran. Only then did the army of Israel pursue them. Saul, therefore, had nothing to lose except David. He knew that if the Lord enabled David to win, the Philistines would accept the results of the battle and either surrender or

[25] Note that neither side was able to conquer the other's hill after a month of fighting (v. 1-16).

run. Had David lost the battle, Saul could still have stood off the Philistines with his army. The fact that the Philistines themselves violated the challenge and ran, rather than surrendering, indicates that the Hebrews likely would have violated it also, since they did not normally even follow the practice. Bringing all this into consideration resolves many of the apparent "problems" in the passage.[26]

Parallels to this type of battle may be clearly seen in many stories of Aegean origin. One might point to the Homerian stories of battles between Achilles and Hector or Livy's account of the champions of the Horatii and the Curiatii.[27] Even Hector's challenge is comparable to Goliath's challenge to Israel.[28] This evidence shows the Aegean origin of the Philistines and their religious beliefs.

Such parallel events are also to be found among the Hittites of Asia Minor, the same area the Trojans later occupied.[29] Hoffer notes that the Hittities often had teams of champions and points to David's twelve men in II Samuel 2:12 as a possible parallel.[30] The Egyptian, Sinuhe, also fought a Syrian foe in such a contest.[31]

The religion and religious practices as well as the history and archaeological artifacts of the Philistines point to their Aegean origin. The "Sea Peoples" were a powerful military movement in Palestine until stopped by men like Samuel and

---

26 Therefore the critical attitude of Albright, *Archaeology and the Religion of Israel,* p. 70, is unnecessary when he doubts the historical validity of the narrative.

27 Cf., quotations given in Erdman, *The Books of Samuel* in Lange (ed.) *Commentary on the Holy Scriptures* (Grand Rapids: Zondervan, n.d.) p. 229.

28 Cf., comments in C. Keil and F. Delitzsch, *Biblical Commentary on the Books of Samuel* (Grand Rapids: Eerdmans, 1950), p. 183.

29 Cf., the extensive discussion in the recent article of H. Hoffer, "A Hittite Analog to the David and Goliath Contest of Champions?" in *Catholic Biblical Quarterly,* xxx, April 1968, pp. 220-25. He says this discovery is the clearest Near Eastern parallel to the David and Goliath contest.

30 *Ibid.*

31 Cf., the text in *ANET,* p. 20 and comments of D. Young, "Sinuhe," *The Biblical World* (Grand Rapids: Baker, 1966), pp. 537-38.

David, whom God raised up to confront them. Their religion was basically foreign to Palestine but they assimilated many Canaanite practices and terms. Israel, however, was little affected or influenced by the religion of the Philistines, though they were much influenced by the Canaanites into whose practices they often apostasized.

III

The Philistines and Archaeology

The Philistine settlement and the influence of their culture was not limited to the coastal plain but stretched far inland to the Shephelah. Not only did they dominate the cities of the pentapolis (Ashdod, Ashkelon, Gaza, Ekron, and Gath) but also such places as Joppa, Jabneel, Gerar, Gezer, Beth-shemesh, and Lachish.[1] Some were found even as far away as Dor.[2] The extensive archaeological findings of Philistine remains testify to their evident influence on culture and politics.

ARCHAEOLOGY AND PHILISTINE MIGRATIONS

In the great "folk movement" of the thirteenth century masses of peoples began to wander from the central plains of Asia and eastern Europe across Europe to the Mediterranean

1 Cf., comments in T. C. Mitchell, "Philistia," in D. W. Thomas (ed.), *Archaeology and Old Testament Study* (Oxford: Clarendon Press, 1967), p. 405. This article is one of the finest brief discussions of the "Philistines" available.

2 Though the Old Testament never mentions them being there, Wen-Amon of Egypt found them there during his travels in c. 1090 B.C. M. C. Astour, *Hellenosemitica* (Leiden: Brill, 1967), p. 8, notes that the people of the Tikara settled at Dor.

Basin and the islands of the sea. The movement brought the Gauls to France, the Galatians to Asia Minor, and the Thraceans to Greece. It resulted in the fall of Troy and the collapse of the Hittite and Hurrian empires (c. 1200 B.C.). The Iron Age began and Assyria rose to power in the Near East while the Greeks were settling the Aegean.[3] During all this mass migration, the Philistines settled on the coast of Palestine.

One-third of the Hittite confederacy that faced Ramses II at Kadesh in 1286 B.C. was the same as the Trojan allies (Dardanians, Mysians, Pedasians, Lycians). The Philistines likely played a part in this war as Hittite mercenaries who had learned metal-working in Anatolia from the Hittites. Albright feels that the Philistines may be identified with the pre-Greek people of the Pelasgians, who allegedly also left Crete with Achaeans, Dorians, Eteocretans, and Cydonians (Odyss. xix, 175-78).[4] This would connect their migrations with the island of Crete. The Philistines pictured in Egyptian monuments do not look like Syrians or Hittites but they do have features similar to the figurations in Minoan and Mycenaean art. Pendlebury notes that the feathered helmet of the Philistines was even used as a hieroglyphic in the famous Phaistos disc of Middle Minoan III.[5] It is possible then, that the Pelasgoi could ultimately point to an origin on the coast of Illyria or in the region of the Danube because of the affinity of the three-man chariots and the burial practice of cremation.[6] The evidence, however, is quite limited and a positive conclusion is not possible. One thing does appear to be certain, though, and that is that neither Crete nor Cyprus

---

[3] Cf., comments of J. Patterson, "The Old Testament World," in Barclay (ed.), *The Bible and History* (New York: Abingdon, 1960), pp. 73-74.

[4] Cf., W. F. Albright, "Some Oriental Glosses on the Homeric Problem," *American Journal of Archaeology,* liv (1950), pp. 162-76.

[5] Cf., discussion by J. Pendlebury, *The Archaeology of Crete, an Introduction* (London: Burns & Oats, 1939), p. 170.

[6] Cf., Patterson, *op. cit.,* p. 76.

was the original home of the Philistines. They were merely temporary stopping places in Philistine migrations.[7] With the fall of the great Minoan civilization, the Philistines moved on into the Near East.

These secular and military-minded Philistine warriors left no written records,[8] and publicity about them has been left to their ardent enemies. As early as Thutmose III of Egypt there is mention of the coastal cities of Gaza, Ekron, and Gerar, although at that time they were under Canaanite control. Later these cities were under Egyptian suzerainty and finally came under Philistine control.[9] However, it must be noted that Flinders Petrie found "Philistine pottery" associated with Egyptian objects (from the period of Ramses II) and Canaanite pottery of the Late Bronze Age (c. 1240 B.C.) at Beth-pelet (Tell Fara).[10] This would imply that for a time all three groups were contemporaneous in Palestine and would push back at least this far the date of the arrival of the Philistines.

While it is true that the people of Ashkelon conquered by Ramses II of Egypt (c. 1290 B.C.) are represented in Egyptian art as Canaanites (or possibly Hittites) and not Philistines, this does not prove absolutely that there may not have been earlier contacts and brief settlements in this area by early "proto-Philistines." The sculptures of Medinet Habu at Thebes show that the army of Ramses III already in the

---

[7] Note that in Amos 9:7, Cyprus is not represented as the original home of the Philistines just as Egypt was not the original home of Israel. The people involved lived there only temporarily. And it was God who called each to their ultimate destination.

[8] At least none have ever been found. Recent discoveries by Franken at Tell Deir-*alla* of three clay tablets of an unknown script may contain an Aegean or Philistine writing, but exact identifications have not been made. Cf. H. J. Franken, Excavations at Deir-allā, Season 1964," *Vestus Testamentum,* xiv (1964), pp. 417-32.

[9] Cf., J. Garstang, *Joshua-Judges* (London: Constable & Co., 1931), p. 88.

[10] Cf., his *Beth-pelet,* Vol. I (London: British School of Archaeology in Egypt, 1930), p. 5.

thirteen century contained Philistine mercenaries.[11] They must have been captured or enlisted at an earlier time. Thus Garstang was willing to push the date for the arrival of the Philistines back from 1190 B.C. to c. 1230 B.C. (last years of the reign of Ramses II). However, such activity would certainly imply even earlier, initial Philistine excursions into the Near East. The fact that their military and seafaring nature caused them to leave little record of their arrival would help explain the lack of evidence for an earlier contact. For example, most archaeologists admit that the so-called "Philistine" ware was not brought by the Philistines from the Aegean but manufactured locally sometime after their arrival.[12] Could not this establish that in their earlier contacts they left little material remains because they were not permanently settled in the area? In the carvings of Ramses III they are shown riding in ox carts. This would imply the transient nature of their early arrival.

While some Philistine mercenaries were fighting in the army of pharaoh, others were already settled on the Egyptian border, again implying an earlier arrival. Garstang suggests that these may have united with the new wave of invaders.[13] The inscription reads: "The Peleset are hung up in their towns" (which could not be farther north than the Phoenician frontier, which marked the limit of Ramses' preparations).

Ramses III reigned for thirty-one years (1198-1167 B.C.) and in the fifth year of his reign the Libyans with the "Sea Rovers" invaded the delta with the intention of settling there. Meanwhile bands of Philistines and Thekels were raiding the delta river mouths. About three years later the Philistines came by land and sea upon Egyptian Syria and wiped out the

---

[11] Cf., H. Nelson, *Medinet Habu,* Vol. I (Chicago: University of Chicago Oriental Institute, 1924-28), p. 5, fig. 4.

[12] E.g., cf. C. Grant, *Beth-shemesh,* p. 42.

[13] *Op. Cit.,* p. 310.

Close up of the "Sea Peoples" battling the Egyptians

Hittite Empire and pushed on to the Egyptian border. The Egyptian annals read:

> The countries. . . of the northerners in their iles were disturbed . . . Not one stood before their hands, from Hatti, Kode, Charchemish, Arvad, and Alasu they were wasted. (They set up) a camp at Amor (i.e., in Central Syria). They desolated his people and his land like that which is not. They came with fire prepared before them, forward to Egypt. Their main support was Peleset (i.e., Philistine), Thekel, Shekelesh, Denyen and Weshesh. These lands were united, and they laid their hands upon the land as far as the circle of the Earth.[14]

Since both the Egyptian army and their captives included Philistines, it would appear that the Philistines fought on both sides. There is no mention in these records of 'Kharu (inland Palestine), which would indicate that it was not disturbed initially by the coastal movement.[15] Egypt afterwards still laid claim to the area according to the inscription of Herihor. Later the repulsed Philistines settled on the Palestinian coast under Egyptian supervision.

Much is uncertain as to the ultimate origins of these Sea Peoples. On the monuments Philistines appear to be fairer in

---

[14] Quoted in Garstang, *op. cit.,* p. 309.

[15] Cf., W. Phythian-Adams, "Philistine Origins," *Bulletin of the British School of Archaeology in Jerusalem,* ii (1923), p. 20.

complexion and different in physiognomy than Semites and, thus, would seem to be Indo-European. Their western-type armor and the fact that they did not practice circumcision seem to point toward this.[16] In tracing the Philistines to the Aegean area one must note, however, that they do not resemble the Minoan Cretans in armor or facial type, which would imply that they stopped only temporarily at Crete.[17]

The Philistine arms and military organization seem rather to be akin to the Iron Age peoples of the Achaean world (especially of the Homeric Age). They wore laminated body armor and were protected with small round shields. There is evidence of laminated body armor in use on Cyprus in c. 1300 B.C. and round shields such as those used by the Sherdens according to thirteenth century Egyptian carvings were also known earlier in the Aegean world.[18] The great, broad swords of the Sherdens were also used by Aegean peoples and the unique Philistine headdress with its distinctive feathered tiara compares with the classical allusion to the Carian crested helmet (Strabo, xiv, li, 327).

This demonstrates at least a Late Bronze Age connection of the Philistines with the Aegean area. This would push their origin back at least two hundred years, making the Philistines similar to early fourteenth century Achaean warriors (cf., those of Homeric legend). The Achaeans were in conflict with the Hattic kings of Asia Minor at that time. This would indicate a measure of movement around the Mediterranean area by the Achaean peoples. Garstang notes that the Philistines were similar in type to those Aegean peoples domiciled for generations on the coasts of Asia Minor. These were later

---

[16] M. A. Meyer, *History of the City of Gaza* (New York: Columbia University Press, 1907), pp. 24-25, was one of the first to emphasize this. He felt the Philistines were of Cretan origin.

[17] Garstang, *op. cit.,* p. 311, saw a possible connection between the Weshesh (Sea People) and the town of Waxos in Crete.

[18] *Ibid.,* pp. 313-14.

Arimaspian figure carved in ivory from Cyprus (c. 1300 B.C.).

swept away by the great migration which left their remnants on the coast of Palestine.[19] He merely draws the conclusion that "proto-Philistines" were mobile in the Mediterranean region prior to their mass migration to Palestine (c. 1200 B.C.). He denies the possibility of their being there earlier.[20] But if Philistine-like people could reach Asia Minor and Cyprus during the Late Bronze Age one must leave the

19 *Ibid.*, p. 315.
20 *Ibid.*, p. 287.

A reconstruction by Gertrude Levy of the Philistines in battle (c. 1190 B.C.). The armor is that depicted at Medinet Habu; the sword is from Gaza; and the shield decorations are taken from early Iron Age "Philistine" pottery.

question of possible "Philistine" contact in Palestine at an earlier time open to further research since the evidence is so limited. Meyer early indicated that these Philistine-like peoples in Asia Minor and Cyprus arrived there from Crete.[21]

Astour, who has made an extensive study of the west Semitic impact on Mycenean Greece, notes that the Medinet

21 *Op. cit.*, p. 25.

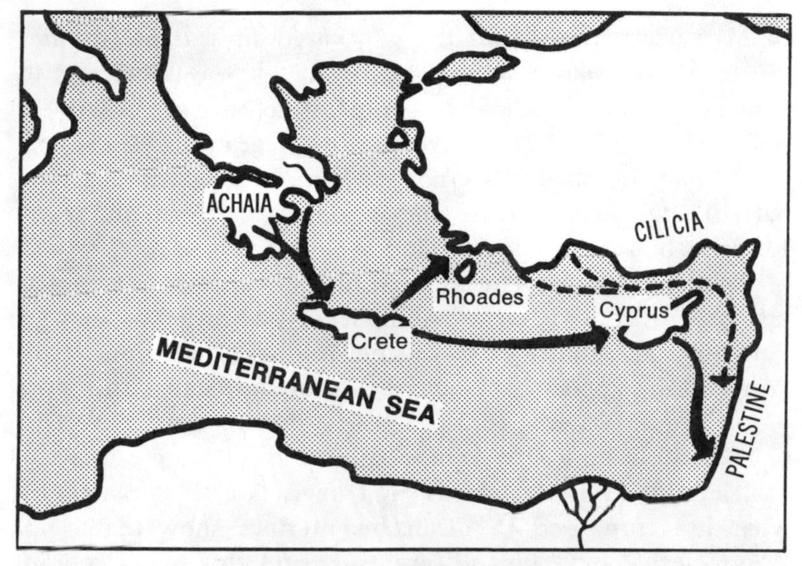

Possible "Philistine" Migrations

Habu inscription says: "The foreign countries made a conspiracy in their islands."[22] He feels that these peoples were probably related to the ʾAgiyawaša-Achaeans of the raid under Merneptah.[23] Again, this demonstrates the mobility of the Aegean peoples throughout the Mediterranean area. He criticizes Albright and Hanfmann for neglecting the fact that the Danuna Greeks are attested in the Amarna letter of Abimilki two centuries earlier.[24] This again substantiates the fact that not all Aegean peoples were foreign to the Near East prior to the mass arrival of Philistines in c. 1200 B.C. Greek contact with Asia Minor at this time was actually far less than with Palestine! In Cicilia there is little archaeological evidence

---

22 Cf., Astour, *op. cit.*, p. 8 ff. For a photo (plate 46) and translation see W. Edgerton and J. Wilson, *Historical Records of Ramses III: The Texts of Medinet Habu*, 2 vols. (Chicago: University of Chicago Press, 1936).

23 *Op. cit.*, p. 8.

24 *Ibid.*, p. 15.

of Mycenaean pottery in the excavated sites at Mersin and Tarsus.[25] The reason appears to be that it was under Hittite control. Eastern Cilicia always appears to have been Semitic prior to 1200 B.C. The movement of Aegean peoples, then, would have touched western Asia Minor but not the eastern part. This would indicate they came from Asia Minor to Palestine by sea, and not by land.

Although Astour denies the Philistine reference in Genesis, he notes that the name of Abimelech is Semitic but that of Phicol is not. *ʾabîmelek* ("my father is king") is a Semitic title rather than a personal name.[26] Astour shows that the term *pî-kôl* ("dark water") is also a title rather than a name. The Greek transliteration *phikola* was made into a name (Poililеô) by Herodotos.[27] He admits that he is not able to discern what it is supposed to mean but it does show that both "Abimelech" and "Phicol" are titles and this may account for both Abraham and Isaac meeting persons with the same names at Gerar.

Even earlier extensive contacts between East and West are substantiated. In tracing ancient civilizations, G. V. Childe notices that Minoan metalurgy had contact in Egypt and Phoenicia as early as the third millennium B.C.[28] There is also evidence of Syrian colonization in Minoan Crete. Not only were the "Sea Peoples" moving east, but, as Astour clearly shows, the Near East was also moving west.[29] Cretans and Egyptians practiced similar burial customs. There is also evidence of sea voyages across the Mediterranean by Syro-Phoenicians as early as the second millennium B.C. and an

---

25 *Ibid.*

26 Cf., T. C. Mitchell, "Philistines," in J. Douglas (ed.), *New Bible Dictionary* (Grand Rapids: Eerdmans, 1962), p. 990.

27 *Op. cit.*, pp. 126-27.

28 Childe, *New Light on the Most Ancient East* (New York: Grove Press, 1957), p. 157 and 177.

29 *Op. cit.*, p. 325.

Akkadian vocative inscription found at Cythera, contemporary with Ugarit II, confirms the trade route.[30] This, along with the mention of Kaphtor (*kap-ta-ra*) in the Mari documents, confirms relations between Crete and Mesopotamia via the cities of the north Syrian coast.

There are extensive examples of contacts between the Aegean and the Near East long before 1200 B.C. People living in Achaea, Crete, and Cyprus bear resemblance to the Philistines long before their major migration to Palestine. All these things point out that it is unfair to pass off the patriarchal references to the "Philistines" as a completely unwarranted anachronism. If Aegean peoples were moving freely about the Mediterranean area even in the third millennium B.C., it is possible that a group of early or "proto-Philistines" landed temporarily, for trading reasons, on the Palestinian coast and had contact with Abraham and Isaac.[31]

PHILISTINE CITIES AND EXCAVATION SITES

The Philistines settled the Palestinian coast in a pentapolis of five city-states and then began to push inland into the Shephelah where they were in conflict with the Hebrews. Although many Philistine sites were first excavated back at the turn of the century, some of the most important work (e.g., Ashdod) is only now being undertaken. The following survey will acquaint the reader with the work done at the more important sites.

1. Ashkelon

Ashkelon (*ʾăšqᵉlon*) was probably an ancient city on the Palestinian coast long before it became a part of the Philistine

---

30 Cf., G. Gossin, *"Les archives economiques du palis de mari," Syria,* xx (1939), pp. 105-26.

31 Cf., comments of D. Kidner, *Genesis, an Introduction and Commentary* (Chicago: Inter-Varsity Press, 1967), p. 142.

pentapolis. Pearlman and Yannai note that the fertile agricultural situation caused it to be a densely populated area even in ancient times.[32] It later became an important seaport and trading center. First built in the third millennium B.C., it was under Canaanite control when mentioned in the nineteenth century B.C. "Execration Texts." The King of Egypt cursed the King of Ashkelon (and those of Jerusalem, Shechem, Hazor, and Beth-shemesh) in the text.[33] It is also mentioned in the Amarna Letters where its King Yitia is mentioned.[34]

It lay on the international highway, Via Maris, that led to Egypt. Its agriculture supplied Egypt with cattle, sheep, honey, and oil. Its wine had international fame.[35] During the reign of Ramses II (1294-24 B.C.) it revolted and was conquered by the Egyptian army. A picture of the conquest has been preserved in stone at Karnack in Egypt. The men of Ashkelon definitely appear to be bearded Semites. According to Judges 1:18, the city was taken by the tribe of Judah, but Judah evidently later had to abandon it to the incoming Philistines who captured it in the twelfth century B.C. From here the Philistines were able to conquer the tribe of Dan and push into the Judean Hills.

The first excavations at Ashkelon were carried out under the, then, newly formed British Mandate of Palestine. During the years 1920-21 John Garstang and W. J. Phythian-Adams excavated Ashkelon and Gaza on behalf of the Palestine

---

32 Cf., article on "Ashkelon" in M. Pearlman and Y. Yannai, *Historical Sites in Israel* (London: Alden, 1964), pp. 164-70.

33 Cf., the comment and interpretation of this by S. Abramsky, *Ancient Towns in Israel* (Jerusalem Post Press, 1963), p. 101.

34 Cf., Letter 320 in A.N.E.T., p. 490. The city is called *aš-qa-lu-na* in Akkadian.

35 Cf., article "Ashkelon" in J. McClintock and J. Strong, *Cyclopedia of Biblical, Theological and Ecclesiastical Literature,* Vol. 1 (New York: Harper Brothers, 1891 Reprint. Grand Rapids: Baker Book House, 1970), p. 461.

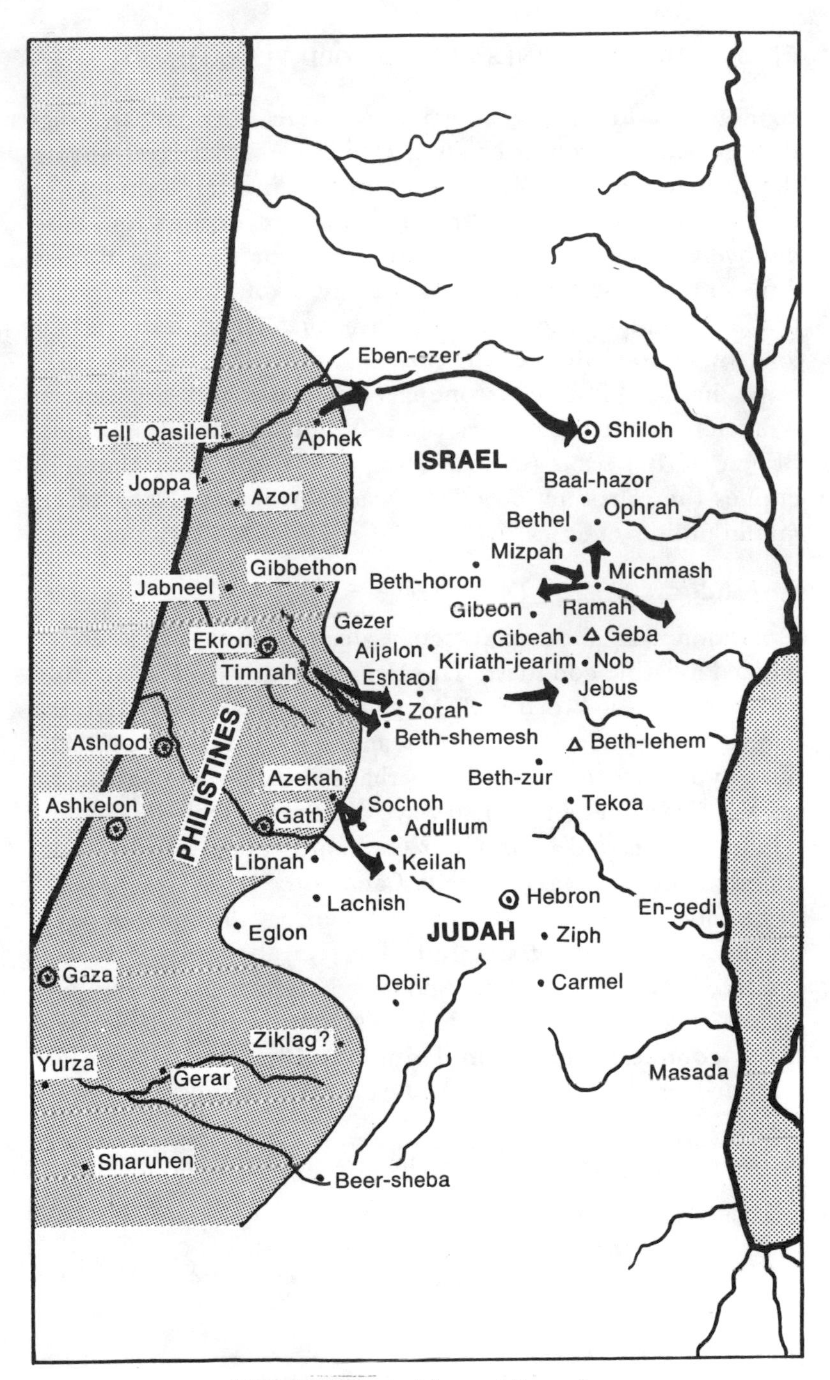

Philistine Cities and Areas of Expansion

Exploration Fund.[36] Though these were not extensive digs they revealed some interesting information. Excavations on the summit cleared only the Roman remains, but sections cut into the mound revealed the succession of occupation. Also discovered was a complete break between the Late Bronze Age and the beginning of the Early Iron Age, which was probably due to the Philistine invasion. They found a new kind of military device: the earth rampart. This massive earth slope had a plastered stone-faced surface and the one at Ashkelon covered an area of 130 acres during the Middle Bronze II B period (c. 1750 B.C.).[37] Yadin feels that this implies the introduction of the war chariot and the battering ram in military tactics.[38]

2. Ashdod

Ashdod was another ancient Canaanite city that later fell under Philistine conquest. The Hebrew name *ʾašdōd* means a "stronghold" or "fortress." Much debate has centered on the name. In Assyrian it is *as-du-du* and in Ugaritic, *áš-da-di*. The old Egyptian form was *ʾisdd* (perhaps thus the modern name isdud). Cross and Freedman have concluded that the Hebrew *Ašdōd* was derived from older Canaanite *ʾaṯdādu*, substantiating that the city was originally Canaanite.[39]

Founded in about the sixteenth century B.C. Ashdod sits on the summit of a grassy hill fifty feet above sea level near the Mediterranean coast, midway between Ashkelon and Ekron. Though it was alloted to the tribe of Judah it was never conquered by them (Josh. 15:46). The Anakim are recorded as living there in Joshua 11:22 and were probably

[36] Cf., the articles by Garstang in the *Palestine Exploration Fund Quarterly Statement,* liii (1921), pp. 12-16, 73-90, 162-9; liv (1922), pp. 112-19; liv (1923), pp. 60-84.

[37] Cf., plan in Garstang, *Joshua-Judges,* p. 358.

[38] Cf., his article in *B.A.S.O.R.,* 137 (1955), pp. 23-32.

[39] F. Cross and D. N. Freedman, "The Name of Ashdod," *BASOR,* 175 (1964), pp. 48-50.

the reason Israel failed to take the city from the Canaanites. It is generally considered to have been one of the greatest Philistine cities and was the place of the temple to Dagon.[40]

The oldest known reference to Ashdod comes from fourteenth to thirteenth century B.C. in the Ras Shamra texts. It refers to a shipment of textiles from Ashdod to Ugarit by a Ugaritic merchant named Šukuna. It indicates a heavy trade with Akko, Ashdod and Ashkelon. The names of the rulers of these cities are generally Semitic, though some, including Widiya of Ashkelon, were Indo-European.[41] The city is also mentioned in the Onamasticon of Amenope (eleventh century B.C.) where it appears as ʾIsdd.[42]

Pottery sherds found on the surface date to the second millennium B.C. and are definitely Canaanite.[43] The Philistines probably settled the town with Egyptian agreement. After the expulsion of the Sea Peoples from Egypt Ramses III settled them in Palestinian strongholds as mercenaries. The Philistines not only had a monopoly on iron but also were making their own steel (iron mixed with charcoal). Metal-smelters found here and at Jamne confirm this factor in their supression of Judah.

No formal excavations of Ashdod were ever undertaken until M. Dothan and D. N. Freedman began work there in 1962.[44] An extensive report of their initial finds was pub-

---

[40] Cf., D. J. Wiseman, "Ashdod," in J. Douglas (ed.), *The New Bible Dictionary* (Grand Rapids: Eerdmans, 1965), pp. 94-95.

[41] Cf., text 311 in *ANET.* The gentilic form *áḏddy* in Ugaritic should be read as *aṯdadiya* ("the Ashdodite"). In the text it also appears with the gentilic forms of *mṣry* ("Egyptian") and *knʿny* ("Canaanite"). Also on *wi-id-ia,* cf., P. Dumont in R. O'Callaghan, *Aram Naharaim* (Rome: Pontifical Biblical Institute, 1948), p. 153, no. 78.

[42] Text in *ANET,* no. 263 in list.

[43] Cf., comments by Abramsky, *op. cit.,* p. 107.

[44] Cf., M. Dothan, "First Season Excavations at Ashdod, 1962," *Israel Exploration Journal,* xii (1962), pp. 147-48; and D. N. Freedman, "The Second Season at Ancient Ashdod," *Biblical Archaeologist,* xxvi (1963) pp. 134-39.

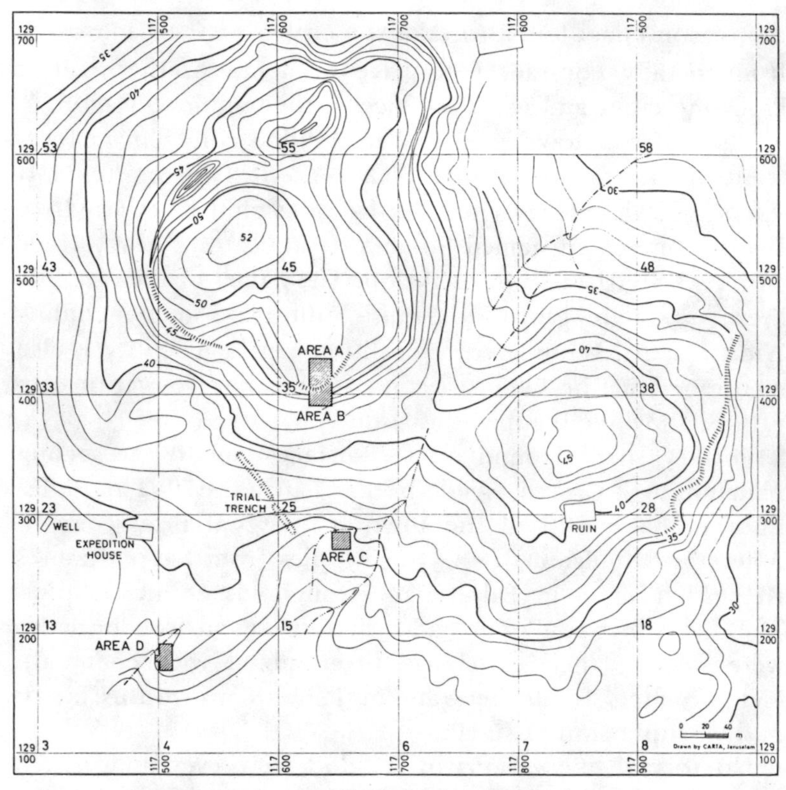

Topographical map of Tel Ashdod and excavation areas

lished in 1967.[45] Further excavations were carried out in 1963 and 1965, but await publication.

The finds from Area A include pottery, lamps, and Rhodian stamps, dated from the middle of the third century B.C.[46] In stratum three were found "fish-plates" of the Hellenistic period.[47] Stratum two also contained several

45 M. Dothan and D. N. Freedman, Ashdod I: *The First Season of Excavations,* 1962 (Jerusalem: Atiqot, 1967). This extensive survey (171 pages plus plates) should be thoroughly consulted by the reader.

46 *Ibid.,* p. 18.

47 *Ibid.,* p. 21.

items from the Hellenistic period and items from stratum one were of the Byzantine era.[48]

In Area B material was found from the Philistine period down to the Byzantine era. Most of the finds were from the Late Bronze Age although ring-base pottery similar to that found at Beth-shemesh was discovered.[49] The excavators also found remains of imported Mycenaean and Cypriote pottery ware dating from the fourteenth century B.C. (prior to the arrival of the Philistines).[50] Stratum two revealed further evidence of imported Mycenaean and Cypriote pottery, clarifying that Ashdod was a substantial trading center along the eastern Mediterranean.[51] Though it is not listed in the Amarna letters, it must have been a large city under Egyptian suzerainty. Finally, in stratum one there is conclusive evidence of the thorough destruction of the city, as well as a transition in pottery forms, at the end of the thirteenth century B.C.[52] This destruction is probably to be attributed to the Philistines since Israel never captured Ashdod. Pottery found in this level is paralleled by other LBA finds at Lachish, Beth-shemesh, Megiddo, and Tell Beit Mirsim.[53] There was even more Mycenaean and Cypriote ware at this level.

The most interesting find was an inscribed sherd of the Iron Age period.[54] The readable letters are *pḥr,* with "p" written with an almost straight horizontal bar and a sweeping curved stroke. Dothan and Freedman suggest that the pot originally bore the name of the potter as well as his profession (*happōḥēr*), which may be the equivalent in the "Philistine" Canaanite dialect of Ashdod to the Hebrew *yōṣēr.*[55]

---

48 *Ibid.,* pp. 27-33.

49 *Ibid.,* p. 76.

50 *Ibid.,* pp. 76-77.

51 *Ibid.,* pp. 80-81.

52 *Ibid.,* p. 81.

53 *Ibid.*

54 *Ibid.,* pp. 84-85.

55 Cf., their extensive discussion of this, *ibid.,* p. 85.

In Area C more Philistine ware was recovered including several beer mugs.[56] The extensive amount of black-on-red-burnished pottery reveals, as expected, Philistine occupation in the early Iron Age.

The second season of excavations produced more light on the Philistine occupation of the site.[57] Altogether twenty levels of the tell were identified, with levels ten to fourteen relating specifically to the Philistines of the twelfth to eleventh centuries B.C.[58] A Philistine fortress was uncovered in Area A. It was built into the wall of the acropolis and dominated the surrounding area. On the north side it was attached by a platform and a sloping ramp.[59] It testifies adequately to the military prowess of the Philistines, who from these maritime fortresses were able to subjugate the whole area. The full plan of the Philistine city is yet to be completely unearthed. In Area D a thirteen-foot thick portion of the outer wall was also discovered. It evidently encircled the lower city and was linked to the wall of the fortress on the acropolis.[60]

Further excavations should reveal even more details of this ancient city of the Philistine pentapolis. It is now the most thoroughly excavated of the major Philistine cities.

3. Ekron

Though this site has never been permanently identified, many feel it is the modern Khirbet al-Muqannaᶜ.[61] Joshua 15:14-46 indicates that it must have been a fairly substantial city, having villages dependent upon it. Surface explorations

56 *Ibid.*, p. 109.

57 D. N. Freedman, *BA*, pp. 134-39.

58 *Ibid.*, p. 136.

59 *Ibid.*

60 *Ibid.*, p. 137.

61 Cf., the reports of J. Naveh, *IEJ*, viii (1958), pp. 87-100, 165-170; and Y. Aharoni, *PEQ*, xc (1958), pp. 27-31.

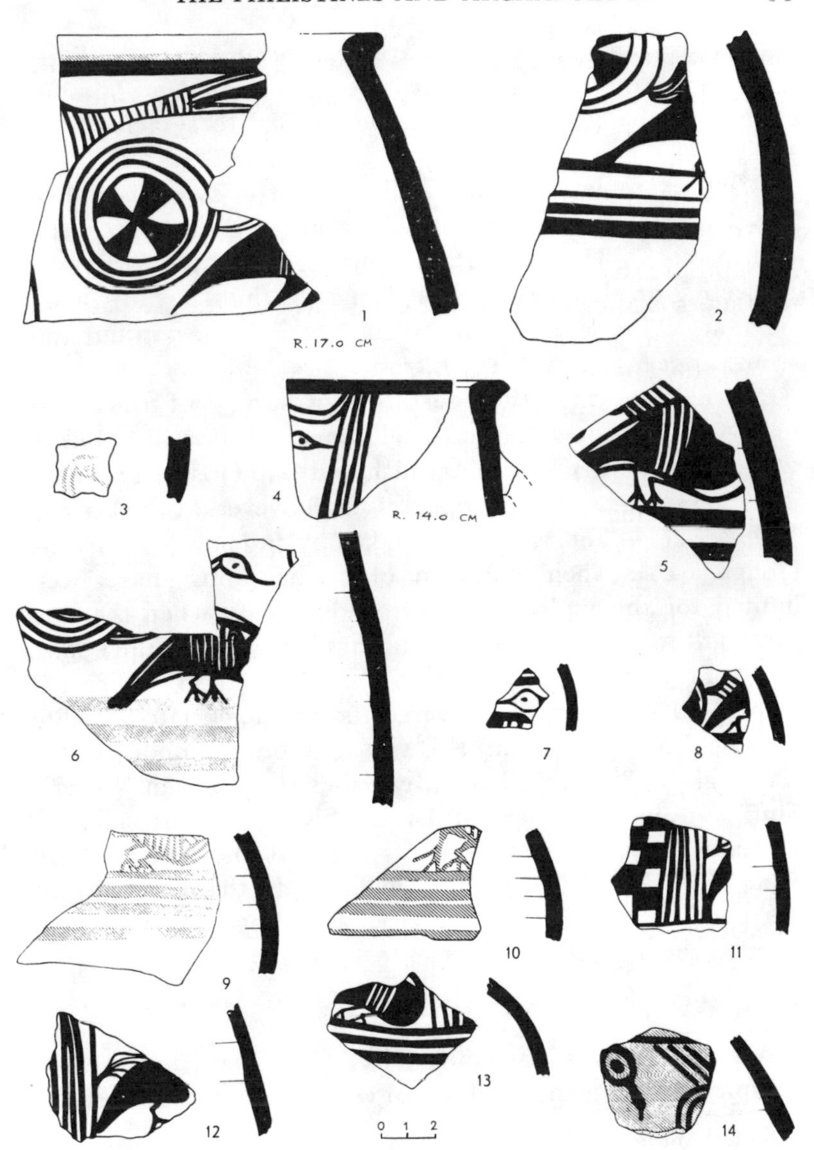

Philistine pottery from Ashdod, Area C

in 1957 revealed the site to have been occupied in the Early Bronze Age but not again until the Early Iron Age. Mitchell notes that the city was walled and covered forty acres at its peak.[62]

Many examples of typical Philistine pottery were found on the site,[63] as well as the double wall, which included gates and towers.[64] There is an acropolis on which the fort stood projecting on the northeastern corner of the tell. Full identification of the site remains to further investigation but this would appear to be ancient Ekron.

Mitchell provides the most helpful survey of the city's history.[65] He notes that in the allotment of the tribes, Ekron was on the border between Judah and Dan (Josh. 15:11, 45, 46; 19:43). It remained unpossessed, however, at the time of Joshua's death and was finally taken by Judah at a later time (Judg. 1:18). Their duration of control must have been limited for the Philistines controlled the city when the captured ark of the covenant was taken there from Gath (I Sam. 5:10). From here they sent it on to Beth-shemesh on a cart (I Sam. 6). Later Samuel delivered the city back into Israelite control (I Sam. 7:14) but this was again only temporary as it was back in Philistine hands by Saul's time (I Sam. 17:52). Thus, for the early part of Israel's history, it was mainly a Philistine city. In later times its god was the famous Baalzebub (II Kings 1:2, 3). This would imply that each city of the pentapolis had its own deity, with Dagon being recognized as the greatest.

4. Gath

Another former Canaanite city, Gath was at one time occupied by the giant Anakim, of whom men like the "Philis-

---

62 T. C. Mitchell, "Ekron," *NBD*, p. 355.

63 Cf., Naveh, *op. cit.,* p. 87 f.

64 Cf., Aharoni, *op. cit.,* p. 30.

65 *NBD*, pp. 354-55.

tine" Goliath may have been descendants. The people of Gath are called "Gittites" (*gittî* or *gittîm*) in Joshua 8:3. The Gittites occupied an important place in early Israelitish history. They received the ark of the covenant when it was removed from Ashdod and were struck with what many consider to be a bubonic plague.[66] David later fled there from Saul and ultimately struck a relationship with Achish, king of Gath while he was a fugitive from Israel (I Sam. 27). Still later David added the city to his realm (I Chron. 18:1) and maintained both Gittite friends (II Sam. 6:10, 11) and mercenaries (II Sam. 15:18). Since Uzziah (II Chron. 26:6) conquered it from the "Philistines" it is possible that it had remained in a loose vassalage to Judah over the years.

The actual site of Gath has never been identified with certainty. An expedition by the Israel Exploration Society under Yeivin began excavating Tell el-ʿAreini (twenty miles north of Gaza) in 1956 supposing it to be ancient Gath.[67] However, further investigations have indicated it is unlikely that this site is ancient Gath.[68] ʿAraq el-Men shîyeh and Tell en-Nağila[69] also may very well be the site of ancient Gath, though positive identification cannot be made without further investigation. Wherever the Philistine town was, its name meant "winepress," it was the furtherest inland of the Philistine cities, bordering Israel on the edge of the Shephelah.

---

66 Cf., T. C. Mitchell, "Gath" in *NBD*, p. 454.

67 Cf., S. Yeivin's articles in *IEJ*, vi (1956), p. 258-59; vii (1957), pp. 264-65; x (1960), pp. 122-23.

68 Although Albright still favors Tell el-ʿAreini, Yeivin now feels it is *Mmšt* (cf., Thomas, pp. 219 f.). Cf., his *Excavations at Tell "Gath," 1956-58* (Jerusalem: Israel Exploration Society, 1961), pp. 10 f.

69 Cf., R. Bulow and R. A. Mitchell, "Report of the Excavations at Tell en-Nağila," *IEJ*, xi (1961), pp. 101-10; and a later report in *BA* xxvi (1963), pp. 30 f.

5. Gaza

Gaza is the most southwesterly town in Palestine and was also an ancient Palestinian city. It was a Canaanite border city before the time of Abraham. The Hebrew name *ʿazāh* appears as *Ga-da-tu* in Egyptian, as in Arabic where the *ʿa* changes to a *ghayin* (also in the Greek, *Gaza*). In Akkadian, though, the *a* form is retained as *Azzati* in the Tell el-Amarna letters and as *Ḫa-az-zu-tu* in later Assyrian.[70] Deuteronomy 2:23 indicates it was originally inhabited by the Av̌v̌im who were driven out by the Caphtorim (proto-Philistines). It appears to have passed from Amorite to Hyksos to Canaanite control. In the Amarna letters Gaza is mentioned and its Canaanite King, Yabriti is referred to as being educated in Egypt.[71]

Albright feels that the Egyptians had their main administrative center of Palestine at Gaza.[72] Joshua conquered it while it was under Canaanite control with some Anakim remaining there (Josh. 10:41; 11:21). However, Israel lost the city again during his lifetime (Josh. 13:3) to the Philistines. It was later the scene of Samson's exploits and finally his death (Judg. 16). The pillared building with spectators on the roof, which he pulled down, has some features parallel to Cretan architecture.[73]

It is difficult to identify the actual site of Gaza, though it is most probably Tell el-ʿAjjul which lies two miles from the coast and six miles south of the modern city of Gaza. The British School of Archaeology in Egypt excavated this spot at the mouth of the Wade Ghazzeh between 1930 and 1934

---

70 Cf., discussion by M. A. Meyer, *History of the City of Gaza* (New York: Columbia University Press, 1907), p. 4. The *ʿayin* of Hebrew is often Ḫ in Akkadian; cf.*ʿomri* with *Ḫu-um-ri-ia*.

71 Cf., J. Knudzon, *Die El-Amarna-Tafeln* (Berlin, 1908-15), pp. 1342, 1575. Name appears in a list with the city (*az-za-ti*).

72 See his comments in *Cambridge Ancient History*, ii, ch. xx, p. 7.

73 Cf., T. C. Mitchell, "Gaza" in *NBD*, pp. 454-55.

under Sir Flinders Petrie.[74] He uncovered five occupation levels from the Middle and Late Bronze Age buildings, but nothing was found to confirm that the site was actually ancient Gaza, though it probably is. He found a cemetery of MB I that lay beneath a palace (?) belonging to MB II.[75] Four other large buildings succeeded it of which the last probably belongs to the Early Iron Age.[76] Substantial pottery remains were found from the Philistine period.[77] The maximum expansion of the MB city included a great fosse of the Hyksos-type.[78] Albright has also indicated that because of the appearance of pottery and weapons of the EB phase the town was occupied even earlier.[79] One of Petrie's interesting finds was pottery from the sixteenth century B.C. beautifully painted with geometric designs and animals.[80]

Since the new site of modern Gaza is still occupied little excavation may be done there. It was rebuilt in 57 B.C. on this spot nearer to the sea by Gabirius. W. J. Phythian-Adams attempted trial excavations there in 1923 but was unable to recover much material.[81]

6. Beth-shan

Important excavations of Philistine remains have come from many sites other than the Philistine pentapolis. Beth-shan, for example, has revealed some very important remains

---

[74] The report of his discoveries may be found in F. Petrie, *Ancient Gaza,* 4 vols. (London: British School of Archaeology in Egypt, 1931-34).

[75] Cf., Petrie, *op. cit.,* I, p. 30 ff. K. Kenyon, *Archaeology in the Holy Land* (New York: Praeger, 1965), p. 307, implies this identification may be somewhat questionable. Her survey of the site is very helpful.

[76] So Kenyon, *ibid.*

[77] *Ibid.,* p. 230.

[78] Cf., Petrie, *op cit.,* III.

[79] W. F. Albright, "The Chronology of a South Palestinian City," *American Journal of Semitic Languages and Literature, lv (1938), pp. 337-59.*

[80] A. Heurtley in *QDAP,* viii (1939), pp. 21-37.

[81] Mitchell, "Gaza," *NBD,* p. 455.

of Philistine culture. The city sits at the junction of the Valley of Jezreel with the Jordan Valley. The name appears in the Old Testament as both *Bêṯ šeʾān* (Josh. 17:11) and *Bêṯ šan* (I Sam. 31:10). They are obviously the same place, however. The modern village of Beisan stands adjacent to Tell el-Ḥosn, the site of the ancient city. The excavation of the city was headed by C. S. Fisher (1921-23) for the University of Pennsylvania. Alan Rowe took over as field director from 1925-28 and he was followed by G.M. Fitzgerald (1930-33). After 1933 the excavation was discontinued.[82]

The lowest level reached dates from about the fourteenth century B.C. The major work centered in an area containing a series of superimposed temples (beginning in the Early Iron Age) and succeeded by a Hellenistic temple and a Byzantine church. Pottery was found dating all the way from the Chalcolithic period and the Early Bronze Age. A deep sounding was made revealing settlements back to the fourth millennium B.C. but the excavators were not able to continue digging in that deep and concentrated a fashion on the nine upper levels.[83] Mitchell indicates that during this earlier period the city was an Egyptian fortified outpost.[84] In the fifteenth century Thutmose III mentions it as being under his control and in the following century it was mentioned in the Amarna letters as the Egyptian garrison *bît-sa-a-ni.*[85] The Canaanite city that was unearthed has been fortified with

82 The most helpful survey of the results of this excavation is G. M. Fitzgerald's "Beth-shan" in D. W. Thomas, *OATS,* 1967, pp. 185-96. The original excavation reports are in four volumes: A. Rowe, *Beth-shan I: The Topography and History of Beth-shan,* 1930; *Beth-shan II, i: The Four Canaanite Temples of Beth-shan,* 1940; G. M. Fitzgerald, *Beth-shan II, ii: The Pottery,* 1930; G. M. Fitzgerald, *Beth-shan III: Excavations 1921-23, the Arat and Byzantine Levels,* 1931; G. M. Fitzgerald, *Beth-shan IV: A Sixth Century Monastery at Beth-shan,* 1931. All published for the University Museum by the University of Pennsylvania Press at Philadelphia.

83 Cf., Rowe, *Beth-shan I,* pp. 10 f.

84 T. C. Mitchell, "Beth-shan," *NBD,* p. 145.

85 *Ibid.*

double walls and the inner and outer walls connected with cross walls which formed small rooms. The fortifications further included a tower built with large unbaked bricks on a foundation of basalt blocks.[86]

They found a temple in Level IX dedicated to "Mekal, the Lord (Baʿal) of Beth-shan." In it they recovered the remains of a three-year-old sacrificed bull. They also found two royal stelae of Seti I which refers to the ʿApiru peoples.[87] In Level VII they uncovered a temple in which was a stela depicting a goddess with a two-horned headdress that is probably Ashtoreth. In the next level they found a temple of the time of Ramses III. Rowe feels that in c. 1187 B.C. soldiers of Ramses III came to Beth-shan to erect a statue to their master.[88] On the left shoulder was the cartouche of his title: "Lord of Two Lands" and his throne name: "Powerful-of-truth-is-Ra; beloved of Amen." On the right shoulder was his personal name: "Ramses-ruler-of-Heliopolis." Père Vincent feels that mercenaries took the citadel for themselves after Ramses' death (c. 1167 B.C.) and later they amalgamated with the incoming "Philistines."[89] Rowe feels that the north and south temples found from this time are probably those of Dagon and Ashtoreth (cf., I Chron. 10 and I Sam. 31).[90] He also indicates that both temples of the Ramses period fell into Philistine hands.[91] Also Serpent Stones were found there that were used in religious practices of the temple.

---

86 Cf., the survey by J. Finegan, *Light from the Ancient Past* (Princeton: Princeton University Press, 1959), p. 167.

87 W. F. Albright, "The Smaller Beth-shan Stele of Sethos I," *BASOR* 125 (1952), pp. 24-32.

88 Cf., Rowe, Beth-shan I, p. 38. (cf., also picture).

89 Cf., his early article in *RB* (1928), p. 436.

90 *Op. cit.*, pp. 40-41. He criticizes those who denied the validity of the Biblical text.

91 Cf., *Beth-shan II*, pp. 22-35, for his most detailed discussion of these temples, including diagrams, etc.

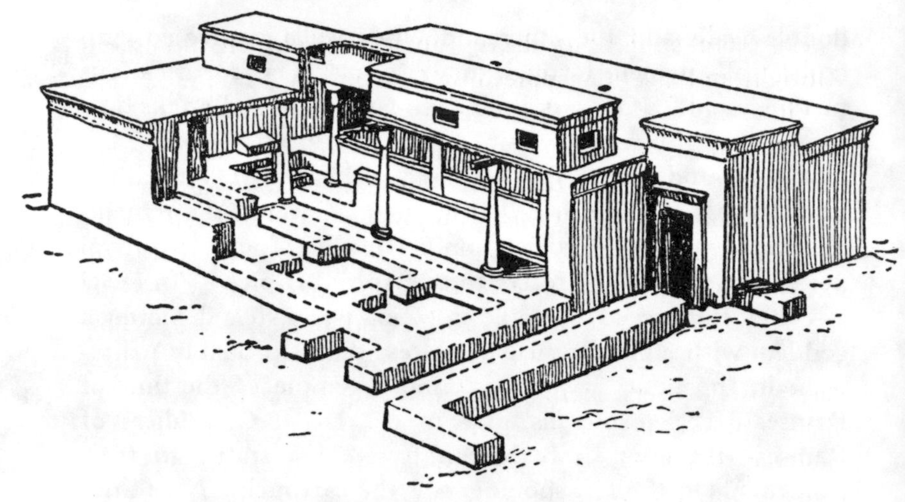

Southern Beth-shan Temple ("Temple of Dagon")

Northern Beth-shan Temple ("House of Ashtoreth")

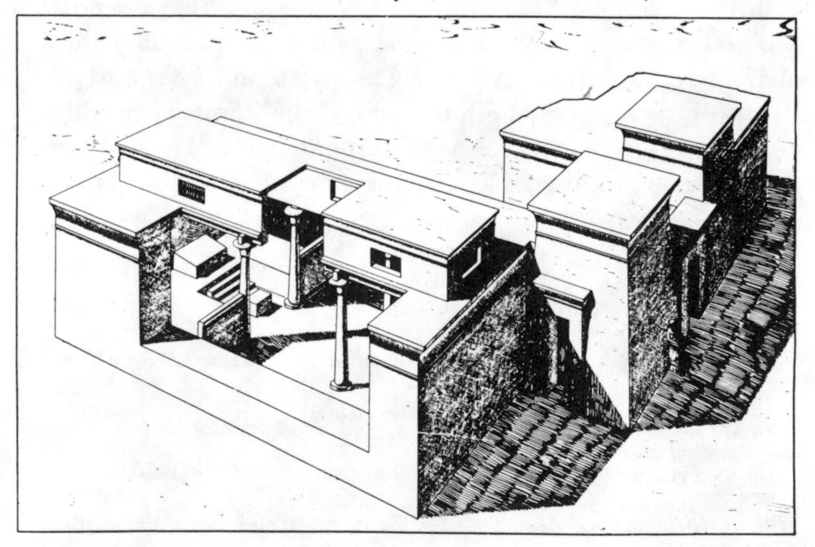

These were similar to those found at Tell Beit Mirsim by Albright and at Beth-shemesh by Grant.[92]

Fitzgerald suggests that there were relations between the "Sea Peoples" and the native Canaanite population at an early time and thus the Philistines, after their victory on Mount Gilboa, exposed the bodies of Saul and his sons on the city wall there (I Sam. 31:10-12).[93] In relation to this the excavators found evidence of Philistine mercenaries at Beth-shan. In 1922 C. S. Fisher discovered nearly a dozen clay sarcophagi in the northern cemetery of Beth-shan.[94] These clay coffins were similar to some found in Egypt at Tell el-Yahudiyeh, Tell Nebesheh, Saft el-Henneh (in Delta), and el-Gerzeh. The Egyptian examples also had Aegean and Cypriot pottery with them.[95] Thus Wright argues that both those in Egypt and the ones in Palestine were made by hired Philistine mercenaries employed to protect the Egyptian borders.[96] The pottery indicates their Aegean origin and substantiates their earlier existence.

The coffins were cylinders of baked clay, large enough for a body. A portion of the lid was cut out of the coffin so that it was like a huge slipper. On the lid the head, hands and arms of the deceased were formed in high-relief by molded clay.[97]

The Beth-shan coffins were found in rectangular tombs which contrast to the more round Canaanite tombs of this period.[98] A number of scarabs found with the body showed the deceased to have been influenced by Egyptian customs. However, there was evidence of Mediterranean influence also.

---

92 Rowe, *Beth-shan, I,* p. 41.

93 *AOTS,* p. 185.

94 Rowe, *Beth-shan I,* p. 39.

95 *Ibid.*

96 Cf., the extensive survey by G. E. Wright, "Philistine Coffins and Mercenaries," *Biblical Archaeologist,* xxii (1959), pp. 54-66. His original approach to the problem has generally been well accepted.

97 *Beth-shan I,* p. 39.

98 This is Wright's observation, *op. cit.,* p. 55.

Pottery anthropoid coffin with movable lid found at Beth-shan

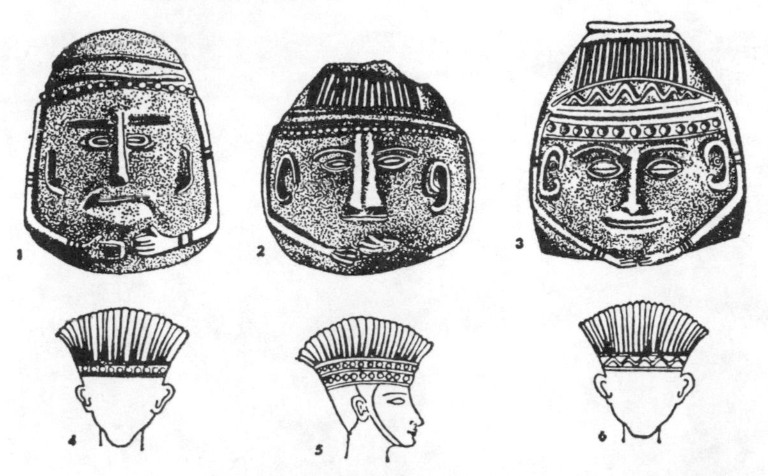

Philistine coffin lids from Beth-shan

The coffins contained "stirrup" vases, lentoid flasks, and other Aegean pottery. The archaeologists also found a lozenge-shaped gold foil mouthplate tied over the corpse's mouth. Similar mouthplates have been found in Cyprus and Aegean sites at Mycenae in Greece.[99] Representations of Egyptian deities were also found, showing the Philistines were very eclectic in religion.

Other clay coffins were found at Tell el-ʿAjjul (Gaza?), Sahab in Trans-jordan, Lachish, Hazor, and Tell el-Farʿah.[100] However, there is a scarcity of "Philistine" pottery with these coffins. The feathered headdress representation on the coffins certainly indicates they are Philistine but many feel the "coffin-people" were not Philistines of the pentapolis but "relatives" who had not yet settled in the area to begin making their own pottery. Thus they had to rely on what they had brought with them. James feels that these proto-"Philistines" of Beth-shan united with Philistines living tem-

99 *Beth-shan I*, pp. 39-40.

100 Wright, *op. cit.*, pp. 56-59.

Anthropoid coffin lid from a Philistine tomb at Tell Fara

porarily in a garrison at Gilboah to overthrow Saul. Thus he feels that I Chronicles 10:8-12 and I Samuel 31:8-13 may be harmonized by realizing that the Israelites identified both as "Philistines."[101] Wright supports this saying that the Hebrew word for "Philistines" was used by the Israelites for all "Sea Peoples" because the Philistines were the dominant group in Palestine.[102] This means that the Genesis reference, though admittedly early, is not necessarily inaccurate if the term "Philistine" had been inserted to more clearly identify an early related group who temporarily landed on the Palestinian coast. Also the clay coffins in Tomb 570 at Lachish must give evidence of an early appearance of the coffin-people in Palestine before the Israelite conquest.[103]

---

[101] F. James, *The Iron Age at Beth Shan* (Philadelphia: University of Pennsylvania Press, 1966), p. 137. His survey is very helpful and thorough.

[102] *Op. cit.,* p. 59, n. 10.

[103] *Ibid.,* p. 66.

The conclusion on the anthropoid coffins is that the Philistines made those found in Egypt, Nubia, and Palestine where they were mercenaries guarding the northern and southern borders of Egypt. They apparently adopted the custom from the Egyptians, modifying their practices with some of their own Aegean traditions.

7. Beth-shemesh

This Judaean city was some twenty miles west of Jerusalem with its northern border in Dan, overlooking a route from the hill country to the coastal plain. The excavations at Beth-shemesh were conducted at the site of ʿAin Shems on the south side of the Valley of Sorek, near the old Philistine territory. During 1911 and 1912 Duncan MacKenzie began excavating there for the Palestine Exploration Fund.[104] The main series of excavations came in 1928-32 sponsored by Haverford College in Pennsylvania, and directed by Elihu Grant.[105]

MacKenzie's findings at the site included evidence of Aegean and Cypriot pottery in the Late Bronze Age city.[106] He felt it may have been brought there by early "Philistine" traders. Grant found that the city was destroyed in the tenth century B.C., probably by the Egyptian King Sheshonk.[107] The original site, however, had been settled in c. 2000 B.C. as a flourishing Canaanite city. He also found a clay tablet there written in the Ugaritic cuneiform alphabet.[108] Mitchell feels that the abundance of Philistine pottery there shows that

---

104 Cf., D. MacKenzie, "Excavations at ʿAin Shems," *Annual Report of the Palestine Exploration Fund,* i (1911), pp. 41-94; ii (1912), pp. 1-100.

105 See his reports in *Beth-shemesh* (Haverford: Haverford Archaeological Expedition, 1929); *Ain Shems Excavations* (Palestine), Part I, 1931, Part II, 1932. Also, E. Grant and G. E. Wright, *Part IV (Pottery),* 1939. The only problem with Grant's reports is that he tends to be unbearably "wordy."

106 *PEF,* i, pp. 41-50.

107 Grant, *Beth-shemesh,* pp. 20 f.

108 *Ibid.*

Philistine vase found at Beth-shemesh (Notice stylized bird at right)

they were well established inland, as well as on the coast.[109] Grant notes that there is no evidence that the Philistines ever disturbed the Canaanite tombs at Beth-shemesh. These included iron fragments of bracelets or anklets, indicating that iron was not initially introduced into Palestine by the Philistines even though they popularized its usage and controlled its manufacture.[110]

109 T. C. Mitchell, "Beth-shemesh," *NBD,* p. 146. For a survey of the Philistine pottery uncovered by Grant see no's. 390, 393, 497 illustrated in *Beth-shemesh* (appendix).

110 *Ibid.,* p. 42.

Some of Professor Grant's early observations were that the Philistines brought old imports with them and later manufactured pottery imitations of what they recalled of Aegean-like pottery.[111] He also was one of the first to indicate that the Philistine mercenaries became merchants later when peace came.

The city must have fallen into Israelite hands later for it was set aside as a levitical city (Josh. 21:16; I Chron. 6:59). It appears to be in their hands in I Samuel 6, when the Philistines sent back the unwanted ark to this city. The casemate walls from the time of David found there may imply that he fortified the city in his own struggles with the Philistines.

8. Tell Fara (Beth-pelet)

About fourteen miles above Tell el-ʿAjjul lies Tell el Farʿa (not to be confused with Tell el Farʿah on the Wadi Farʿah). It is on the Wadi Ghazzeh at the point where it turns into the coastal plain. It was excavated between 1928-30 by Sir Flinders Petrie for the British School of Archaeology in Egypt.[112] Petrie identified the site as Beth-pelet of Joshua 15:27 but Albright prefers it to be Sharuhen.[113] The city levels were marked out from Middle Bronze II to the Iron Age. Despite the problem of identifying the site, a wealth of material was found both on the tell and in the tombs.[114] The greatest find was five tombs rich in Philistine pottery.[115] Petrie found Philistine, Egyptian, and Canaanite

---

111 *Ibid.*

112 The records of the excavation may be found in Petrie's *Beth-pelet,* 2 vols. (London: British School of Archaeology in Egypt, 1930, 1932).

113 Cf., Albright's comments in *The Archaeology of Palestine* (Baltimore: Penguin Books, 1960), p. 53. Any final identification must remain uncertain without further evidence.

114 Cf., *Beth-pelet,* I, pp. 10 f.

115 *Ibid.,* p. 6.

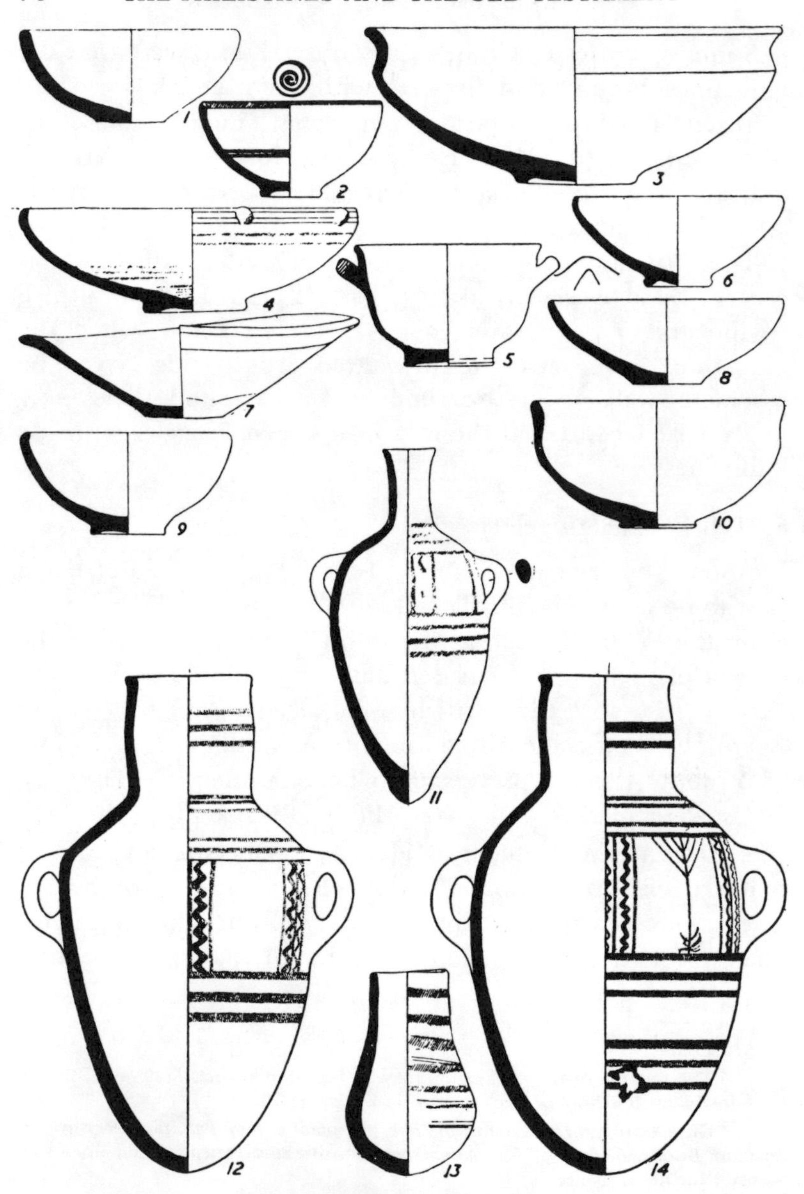

Representation of pottery from the Philistine tombs at Tell Fara

materials side-by-side, indicating temporary coexistence on the site.

Many fine pottery vessels with typical Philistine decorations were recovered as well as evidence of iron weapons. Kenyon notes that this is the first appearance of iron in Palestine that is well authenticated.[116] The tombs, in which these discoveries were made, are not round like the typically Canaanite tombs but rectangular and trapezoidal in shape with steep sides. They are approached by a long, narrow passage. Like the tombs at Beth-shan this implies Aegean influence.[117]

Anthropoid coffins were also found at Tell Fara in two of the tombs. These are similar to those found at Beth-shan (LB 2-EI 1) and in Egypt (which date as early as 1501-1447).[118] Nearly all of these coffins have Aegean and Cypriot objects associated with them, implying early Aegean contact with the Near East.

9. Gerar

This ancient city (cf., Gen. 10) lay in the Judean foothills. Genesis says it was in the "land of the Philistines" (Gen. 21:32-34). Since there is substantial evidence of early Aegean contact with the Near East, this need not be seen as an unhistorical anachronism. Especially when one remembers that the Hebrew word: *pelistîm* stands for all the "Sea Peoples."[119] There can be no doubt that Gerar was an important city in the time of the patriarchs.

Both W. J. Phythian-Adams (1922) and W. Flinders Petrie (1927) excavated Tell Jemmeh (eight miles south of Gaza)

---

116 K. Kenyon, *op. cit.*, p. 227. She provides a very helpful survey of the finds at Tell Fara in pp. 225-29, including pictures and diagrams.

117 See above, n. 98.

118 This is the date given by Kenyon, *op. cit.*, p. 227.

119 See above n. 102.

supposing it to be Gerar.[120] The city was on the main caravan route to Egypt and there was evidence the inhabitants exacted toll from passing traffic. However, Petrie was unimpressed with the work at Tell Jemmeh and transferred his activities to Tell Fara.[121]

In 1956 D. Alon excavated Tell Abu Hureira about eleven miles southeast of Gaza and suggested it was Biblical Gerar.[122] It sits on the present Wadi esh-Shariʿah and the site was abundant with Middle Bronze Age pottery sherds. Alon showed that Tell Abu Hureira had been inhabited in Chalcolithic times and was continually occupied through every period of the Bronze and Iron Ages indicating it was very prosperous during the patriarchal era.[123] Tell Jemmeh, however, has not been able to conclusively show good MB evidence past the sixteenth century B.C.

At Abu Hureira several smelting furnaces were found giving evidence of Philistine iron-working (cf., I Sam. 13:20).[124] Both copper and iron instruments were found there as well as many beer mugs used for barley beer indicating the Philistines were great drinkers.[125] These factors seem to indicate this site is most likely ancient Gerar.

10. Gezer

Gezer was one of the early sites in Palestine to be excavated in the twentieth century in 1902-05 and 1907-09 by R.

---

[120] Cf., Petrie's excavation reports in *Gerar* (London: British School of Archaeology in Egypt, 1928).

[121] C. Pfeiffer, *Baker's Bible Atlas* (Grand Rapids: Baker, 1961), p. 264.

[122] Cf., report by Y. Aharoni, "The Land of Gerar," *Israel Exploration Journal,* vi (1956), pp. 26-32.

[123] Cf., survey by Mitchell, "Gerar," *NBD,* p. 463.

[124] Aharoni, *op. cit.*

[125] Cf., Albright, *The Archaeology of Palestine,* pp. 114-15. He notes that Samson's "feast" recorded in Judges 16:23 was a "feast with drinking" following Philistine custom.

A. S. Macalister for the Palestine Exploration Fund.[126] Later, small-scale excavations were done there by Alan Rowe in 1934.[127] The evidence shows the site was occupied from Chalcolithic times to the Early Iron Age and later.

From its earliest times, Gezer was a city of importance, lying on the road from Joppa to Jerusalem. It was originally a Canaanite royal city and fortress. It is mentioned in the Tell el-Amarna letters in which its King *Yapahi* writes to Akhenaton.[128] It was conquered by the Egyptians during the Eighteenth Dynasty but later regained limited independence under its own king, Horam. Later Horam was killed in a battle with Israel after Gezer and Lachish had formed a confederacy against the Hebrews (Josh. 10:33). The Israelites, however, failed to occupy the city though it was included in the territory of Ephraim, to whom it paid tribute. The stele of Merenptah (c. 1220 B.C.) of Egypt claims the Egyptians recaptured the city. It did not become an Israelite possession until the time of Solomon, when the pharaoh gave it as a gift to his daughter, Solomon's wife (I Kings 9:16).

Tell Jezer was identified as the site of Gezer as early as the late nineteenth century by Professor Clermont-Ganneau. It is well situated on the lower slope of hills above the coastal plain and guarded the western frontier of the Judean hill country. The city was fortified first with a brick wall and later with a thirteen-foot-thick stone wall.[129] Macalister's excavations there verified the occupation of Gezer by the Philistines in the Early Iron Age. II Samuel 21:18 f. and I Chronicles 22:4 refer to a war between Israel and the Philis-

---

126 His reports are in *The Excavations of Gezer,* 3 vols. (London: Murray, 1912). His stratigraphic methods were good but his knowledge of pottery chronology was very limited and has hindered the interpretation of the materials.

127 Cf., *PEQ,* 1935.

128 For an English translation and evaluation see A. R. Millard, "A Letter from the Ruler of Gezer," *PEQ,* 100 (1965), pp. 140-43. Cuneiform original is Amarna tablet 378.

129 Macalister, *Gezer,* I, p. 10.

Hebrew Calendar from Gezer, detailing the agricultural operations appropriate to each season (tenth century B.C.)

tines at "Gob" which Macalister feels is a corruption of "Gezer." The error in transcription changed the original *gzr* to *gôb*.

He found a spring some one hundred twenty feet below the surface of the ground in a cave. A tunnel was cut to it so that the people of the city could obtain water in time of siege. He also made an interesting discovery on the north side of the city. There he found above a burial cave a row of standing stones each five to ten feet high in a slightly curved line from north to south. Macalister originally regarded the area containing these stones to be a Canaanite "high place."[130] However, Watzinger has suggested effectively that

130 Macalister, *Bible Side-Lights from the Mound of Gezer* (London: Murray, 1906), pp. 57-66.

they were memorial stones to the kings of the city and had no real cultic importance.[131]

Another important find at Gezer was the now famous Gezer calendar. Though it comes from a later time (c. 925 B.C.) it gives a good picture of the agricultural situation in Palestine during the Iron Age. The "calendar" consists of a small limestone slate about four inches long and three inches wide. It appears to be merely a schoolboy's exercise, but it also contains a list of various months and the agricultural work done during each.

The script is written in the older Biblical Hebrew and is very readable. The translation reads:

> His two months are (olive) harvest,
> His two months are planting (grain),
> His two months are late planting;
> His month is hoeing up flax,
> His month is harvest of barley,
> His month is harvest and feasting;
> His two months are vine-tending,
> His month is summer fruit.[132]

The parallel structure might also imply that this was an exercise in writing simple Hebrew poetry, especially since the "penmanship" is done so well. Nevertheless, Gezer proved to be rich in artifacts and shed more "light" on the Philistines. The problem of the excavation of Gezer was that F. J. Bliss directed the excavation before Macalister, and Bliss' approach was primitive by modern stratigraphic methods. Thus many of the buildings uncovered could not be assigned an accurate date.

---

131 C. Watzinger, *Denkmäler Palästinas,* Vol. I (Berlin: 1933), pp. 63 f.

132 Cf., translation in Finegan, op. cit., p. 182. His footnote of the translation, however, is misprinted in the 1963 edition.

11. Tell el-Ḥesi

This site lay on the edge of the coastal plain, due west of Hebron. It was first excavated by Sir Flinders Petrie in 1890.[133] Until this time archaeological work in Palestine was merely "pick and grab" and Petrie was the first to make a serious and scientific approach to the matter of digging up artifacts. Already a veteran Egyptian archaeologist, he chose Tell el-Ḥesi for a trial excavation of six weeks using stratigraphical methods of excavation and linking the Palestinian chronology with that of Egypt. He was sponsored by the Palestine Exploration Fund and revolutionized archaeological methodology. The work was continued in 1892 by F. J. Bliss, who followed the same methods and reached the lowest occupation level (c. 2600 B.C.) and found there a group of copper weapons parallel to those found in an Early Bronze III tomb at Jericho.[134]

Petrie's work here was revolutionary in its ultimate consequences for the science of archaeology in Palestine. His identification of the site as Lachish, however, is no longer accepted, as Tell Duweir has generally been identified as that site.[135] However, as Wheeler points out, Petrie's methods were still far from modern standards even though they were an attempt in the right direction.[136]

Among the important finds at Tell Ḥesi relating to the Philistine period were several sherds of Late Helladic III B

---

[133] His report is in *Tell el Hesy* (London: British School of Archaeology in Egypt, 1891).

[134] Cf., Bliss, *A Mound of Many Cities* (London: British Academy, 1894) for the record of his work. On the parallel weapons see K. Kenyon, "A Crescentric Axehead from Jericho, and a Group of Weapons from Tell el Hesi," *Eleventh Annual Report of the Institute of Archaeology, University of London.*

[135] It was excavated by Wellcome, Marston, and Starkey. The reports (*Lachish I-IV*) were printed by Oxford University Press, 1938, 1940, 1953, 1957.

[136] M. Wheeler, *Archaeology from the Earth* (Baltimore: Penguin Books, 1956), pp. 29-30. He notes that army personnel like Lane Fox and Pitt Rivers were using better methods long before Petrie.

style pottery implying more thirteenth century B.C. contacts with the Aegean peoples.[137] The actual identification of the site is still uncertain, though, it was definitely in Philistine hands and under their influence for some time. Albright feels it is the ancient city of Eglon.[138]

12. Philistine "Finds" at other sites

There is also evidence of Philistine influence at other sites in Palestine. A small number of typically "Philistine" sherds were found at Megiddo in both Strata VII and VI. However, it is so little that Kenyon feels the city was never under Philistine control.[139] Since these warriors turned merchants, the finds could imply some limited trading contact. Since the Philistines were certainly in control of Beth-shan for a while and there was also little Philistine pottery found there, this would indicate that the Philistines held these sites only temporarily and generally lived side by side with the Israelites. The Philistines, however, were probably responsible for the total destruction of Megiddo in c. 1050 B.C.[140] The old Canaanite city was destroyed in the twelfth century (Stratum VII) and was rebuilt in a much inferior manner. Its Late Bronze Age fortifications were gone and the gates and palace were very trivial compared to the older city. Then it too was burned to the ground probably by the Philistines, and lay unoccupied for some time.

Some traces of Philistine ware have also been found at Beth-zur, Bethel, and Tell en-Nasbeh. Tell en-Nasbeh is probably to be identified with the Biblical town of Mizpah where

---

137 Cf., Mitchell, *AOTS*, p. 411.

138 *BASOR*, 17 (1925), p. 7. However, J. Lillie, "Eglon," *NBD*, p. 337 also suggests Tell en-Nejileh or Tell beit Mirsim may be Eglon.

139 *Op. cit.*, p. 229. Cf., also C. Watzinger, *Tell el-Mutesellim* (Leipzig: Hinrichssche Buchlandlung, 1929).

140 Cf., G. E. Wright, *Biblical Archaeology* (Philadelphia: Westminster, 1960), p. 55.

Samuel (I Sam. 7) defeated the Philistines. It was excavated between 1926-35 by F. W. Badè of the Pacific School of Religion, assisted by the staff of the American Schools of Oriental Research.[141] The mound is about seven miles north of Jerusalem. Jar handles found there with the word "Mizpeh" stamped on them in old Hebrew letters led to the identification of the site as Mizpeh of Benjamin (Judg. 20:1). The fragments of Philistine pottery found here were from a time when the city was merely a country village but there was enough to show that the site was occupied in Samuel's day.[142] The excavation also turned up Cyro-Phoenician juglets and Philistine pottery resembling that of Rhodes and Late Mycenae (type LH III c) similar to that found at Gezer with Philistine pottery.[143] Philistine chalices were also found at Mizpah similar to those of Tell el-Farʿah.[144]

Lachish (Tell el-Duweir) was excavated under the direction of J. L. Starkey and later by G. L. Harding and C. Inge after Starkey was murdered there in 1938 by Arabs. Shortly before his death he found two anthropoid clay coffins at Lachish in tomb no. 570.[145] Since Late Bronze Age Pottery was found in connection with the burials these coffins are probably the earliest of those found in Palestine (cf., also Tell el-Farʿah and Beth-shan). This again shows earlier evidence for the arrival of "Philistine"-like peoples, since the coffins at Lachish pre-date those found in Egypt according to Wright's

141 The excavation report was written by C. McCown, *Tell En-Nasbeh,* 2 vols. (New Haven: Yale University Press, 1947).

142 *Ibid.,* pp. 54-61.

143 *Ibid.,* p. 94. Cf., also Macalister, *Gezer,* III, pl. 158:15 for a connection between the decoration on a Rhodian vessel and a vessel found at Gezar.

144 *Ibid.,* p. 95.

145 See the excavation report in O. Tufnell, *Lachish IV: The Bronze Age* (London: Oxford University Press, 1958), pp. 36, 131-32, 248-49 with vols. XLV and XLVI. She gives them a late date (early twelfth century B.C.) but Wright, *BA,* xxii (1959), p. 58, suggests that the early thirteenth century is more correct in corresponding with the Late Bronze Age pottery found there.

estimates.[146] The coffins, like those found in Egypt, were inscribed with crude Egyptian hieroglyphs which are not decipherable and were undoubtedly not written by an Egyptian. Thus, we have evidence of probably a small group of proto-Philistines arriving somewhat "early" and settling temporarily at Lachish in the Shephelah.

Little pottery of the so-called "Philistine" type was found at Lachish and Tufnell concluded that this was because it was a well-guarded fortress which was not easily conquered. She felt that the Philistines were certainly there, though, since Philistine pottery has been found as far inland as Beth-shemesh and Tell Beit Mirsim.[147] There is, however, some evidence of side-spout strainer jugs that were popular at the time of the Philistine invasion.[148] Tufnell feels that the site was probably abandoned temporarily after this time and later rebuilt as an Iron Age City.[149]

At Shiloh the Israelites had their central shrine during the early years of the nation (Judg. 21:19). In the time of Eli and Samuel the tabernacle and the ark of the covenant remained there (I Sam. 1:9; 3:3). The site was excavated by a Danish expedition from 1926-29 and again in 1932. Hans Kjaer led the work at Tell Seilun (Shiloh) that revealed it had been destroyed by fire c. 1050 B.C. It is virtually certain that this is the destruction wrought by the Philistines when they captured the ark at Shiloh.[150] The Philistines returned the ark to Beth-shemesh later instead of sending it back to Shiloh, implying that Shiloh had been destroyed and no one was there any longer. Even in Jeremiah's day, he told the

---

146 *Ibid.*, p. 58, n. 7. He argues convincingly for a very LBA date at the horizon of the Early Iron Age.

147 *Lachish III*, p. 47.

148 *Ibid.*, p. 320.

149 O. Tufnell, "Lachish," *AOTS*, p. 303.

150 Cf., report by H. Kjaer, "The Excavation of Shiloh, 1929" in *The Journal of the Palestine Oriental Society*, x (1930) pp. 87-114.

people of Israel to go see the ruin that was at Shiloh as a lesson of their false trust in the temple (Jer. 7:12; 26:6).

There were also sites in the "land of the Philistines" which have been excavated but never identified. Mazar has suggested that Tell el-Ǧerišeh is Gath-rimmon, a "suburb" of Gath.[151] Aharoni has identified Tell el-ʿAjjul as Beth-eglaim and Tell Ǧemmeh as Yurza of the Amarna letters.[152] However, the present significance of these sites remains limited, with the exception that both Tell el-ʿAjjul and Tell Ǧemmeh have yielded pottery that is similar to Late Helladic III B style, popular in the Aegean and similar to that also found at Ashkelon, Tell el-Ḥesi and Tell el-Farʿa.[153]

Mitchell shows early Aegean contacts in the Middle Bronze Age through the intermediation of Cyprus, which he feels were preliminary to later, more direct contacts.[154] He notes that the new weapons introduced into Palestine in the MB II B period were the result of Hyksos innovations. Most of Hyksos personal names were Semitic, however, some were originally Hurrian and Indo-European.[155] He feels that perhaps the horse burial at Tell el-ʿAjjul from this period is due to Hurrian influence. His point is to show that non-Semitic peoples were on the maritime coast long before the arrival of the later "Philistines" and could have been easily identified as such by a later insertion in the Genesis text. However, this may not even be necessary since there is clear evidence of actual trade between Crete and Egypt and Syria at the time of the patriarchs.[156] Albright suggests that Abraham was

---

151 Mazar, "Tell el-Gerisheh," *Israel Exploration Journal,* iv, (1954), p. 227.

152 Cf., his survey report in *IEJ,* vi (1956), p. 32.

153 Cf., F. Stubbings, *Mycenaean Pottery in the Levant,* (Cambridge: Cambridge University Press, 1951), pp. 84-86.

154 *AOTS,* pp. 407-409.

155 *Ibid.,* p. 408. However, this evidence is limited.

156 Cf., *ibid.,* and also R. Ehrich, *Relative Chronologies in Old World Archaeology* (Chicago: University of Chicago Press, 1954), pp. 19-22.

living at Gerar at this time, engaged in a donkey caravan trade between Palestine and Egypt.[157] Now, if there were trade contacts between Syria, Egypt and Crete at this time, it is not impossible that Abraham could have had contact with Aegean, proto-Philistines who were temporarily settled at Gerar.

PHILISTINE POTTERY

The pottery types generally called "Philistine" were entirely new to Palestine. They were elaborately decorated with metopes enclosing stylized birds, usually with a back-turned head. They also commonly have friezes of spirals and groups of interlocking semicircles. This motif is common to most Mycenaean pottery of the Late Helladic period and parallels pottery of Rhodes,[158] Cyprus,[159] and Crete.[160] However, the Mycenaean motifs are never in the same combination in "Philistine" ware. The Philistines combined geometric designs with stylized forms of zoomorphic (generally birds) motifs into a bichrome ware that was strictly Philistine.[161] Philistine pottery is found in abundance on the Palestinian coast where the Philistines settled and is only found in limited quantities inland (e.g., Beth-shan, Beth-zur, and Tell en-Nasbeth). That found at Tell en-Nasbeh resembles the pot-

---

157 W. Albright, *BASOR,* 163 (1961), pp. 36-54. Also, J. Gray, "Ugarit," *AOTS,* p. 150, notes that there were Aegean settlements in the Bronze Age on the coast of Syria and at Tell Abu Hawãm in Palestine. Cf., also J. Bérard, *"Philistins et Préhellénes," Revue Archéologique,* xxxvii (1951), pp. 129-42.

158 McCown, *Tell en-Nasbeh,* I, p. 94.

159 W. A. Heurtley, "The Relationship between 'Philistine' and Mycenaean Pottery," The Quarterly of the Department of Antiquities in Palestine, v (1936), p. 109.

160 J. Bensen, "A Problem in Orientalizing Cretan Birds," *Journal of Near Eastern Studies,* xx (1961), pp. 73-84 (includes pictures).

161 Cf., the description given by J. Gray, *The Canaanites* (New York: Praeger, 1964), pp. 102-103 (including pictures).

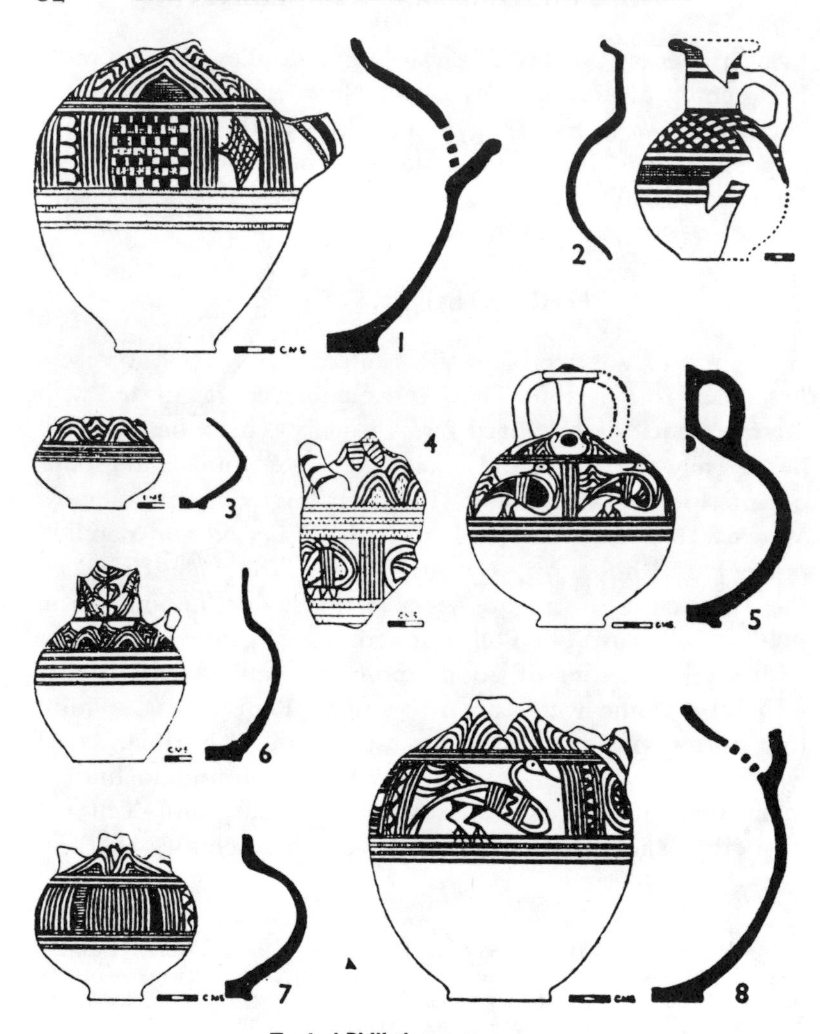

Typical Philistine pottery

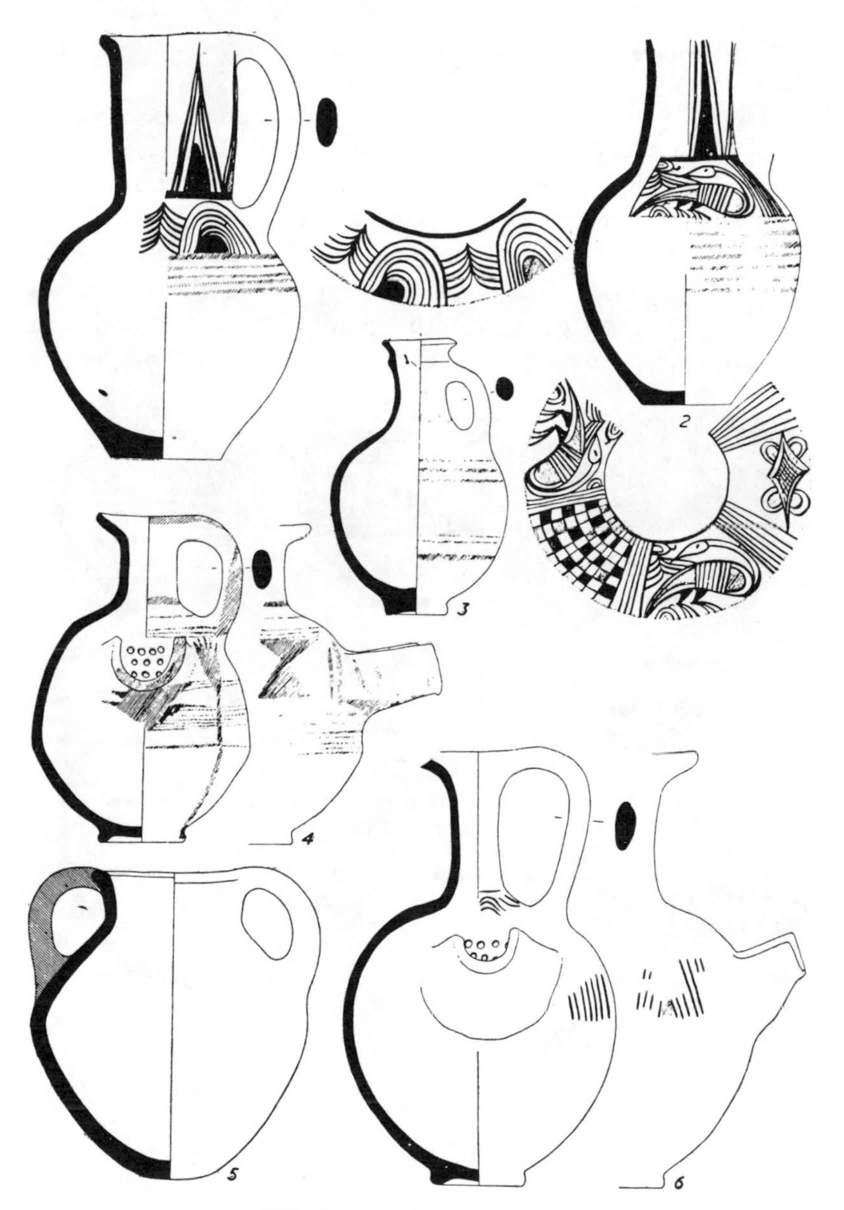

Philistine pottery from Tell Fara

tery of Rhodes and the Late Mycenaean pottery of the LH III c type.[162]

Thus, "Philistine" ware is an ecclectic style based on LH III and was current in the Levant in the last half of the thirteenth century B.C. Kenyon observes that there are Egyptian elements mixed in Philistine pottery also. She suggests that this is due to their contact with Egypt as mercenary soldiers.[163] Therefore, it would appear that the Philistines did not bring this pottery with them but manufactured it in Palestine from memory as an imitation of that which they

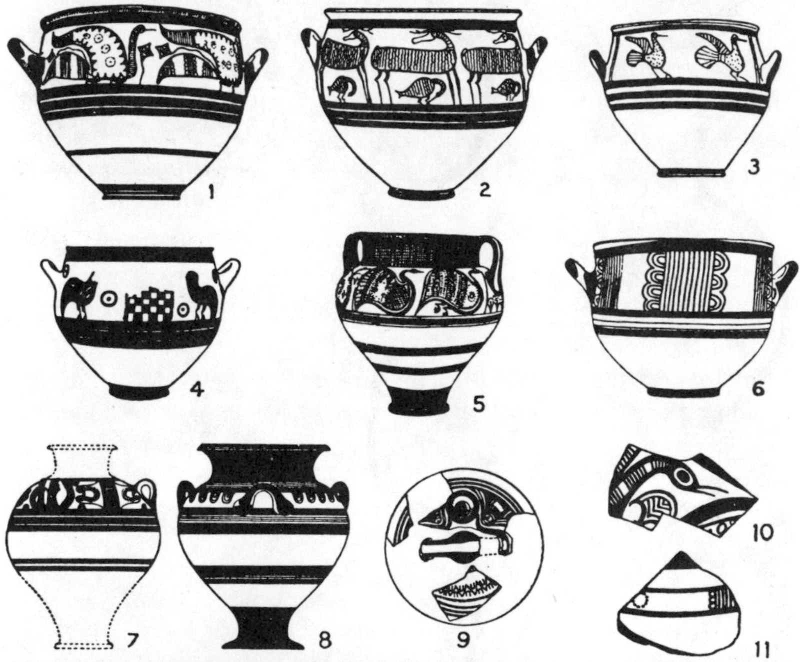

Thirteenth century B.C. pottery: 1-5 Cyrus; 6- Syria; 7-11 Palestine. Notice the similarity of design

162 Cf., McCown, *op. cit.,* p. 94. He notes that LH III c pottery itself appears with Philistine pottery at Gezer, proving the connection. Cf. Macalister, *Gezer,* III, pl. 158:15.

163 *Op. cit.,* p. 224.

knew in their Aegean homeland. Heurtley observes that "Philistine" pottery borrows from all types of Mycenaean ware, not any particular kind, and that it retains Mycenaean elements beyond the period of normal Mycenaean pottery.[164]

The stylistic comparisons between Philistine ware of Palestine and the pottery of Cyprus and Crete completely overlap, so that one may not say that Philistine ware is either definitely Cypriote or Cretan. For example, the bird in the above picture (no. 10) looks Rhodian rather than mainland, while the chariot pieces are probably Cypriot.[165] The krater from Minet el Beiḍa in Syria has concentric arcs similar to those on Philistine pottery (cf., no. 6 above). Heurtley feels that this implies Philistine contact with Mycenaean culture and then Philistine assistance in spreading it East.[166] Recent discoveries by Mazar at Tell el-Qasileh on the northern outskirts of Tel Aviv show extensive Philistine pottery at a site far north of any previously found.[167] Wright suggests that Strata XII-XI at Tell el-Qasileh contains the best examples of Philistine ware, while Stratum X, which is contemporary with Megiddo VI and Tell Abu Hawām IV B, has a much poorer remnant of the finer Philistine painted pottery.[168] This is exactly the time when Philistine power had reached its zenith and began to decline. It would seem, then, that the Philistines penetrated the northern area at an early time and later lost their influence and control there.

---

164 *Op. cit.*, p. 109. He suggests calling it "Derivative LH III" but admits the title is too clumsy to become popular. The term "Philistine" ware is undoubtedly better. This is also Albright's opinion, *The Archaeology of Palestine*, p. 114.

165 For other Mycenaean pottery found at Tell Abu Hawam cf., *QDAP*, iv (1935), pp. 45-54 and Plates XVII, XIX-XXII.

166 *Op. cit.*, p. 97.

167 *IEJ*, i (1950-51), pp. 61-76, 125-40.

168 G. E. Wright, "The Archaeology of Palestine," in G. E. Wright (ed.), *The Bible and the Ancient Near East* (Essays in Honor of William Foxwell Albright). (Garden City: Doubleday, 1961), pp. 116-17.

Fourteenth and thirteenth century B.C. pottery from Crete

The zoomorphic designs of birds on Philistine pottery seem to parallel most closely those of Cretan pottery. The stylized representations of the birds have the same basic characteristics as those on Philistine pottery. Probably the closest parallel is between Philistine ware and Mycenaean III C 1 b style pottery found at Sinda and Enkomi in eastern Cyprus by Furumark.[169] This pottery is almost identical with the earliest Philistine ware found in Palestine. This Cypriote pottery, in turn, resembles the Mycenaean ware of Argos in Greece.

Most authorities feel that the actual "Philistine" pottery was not made in the Aegean and brought to Palestine, but

169 The excavations were carried out by the help of C. F. A. Schaeffer and P. Dikaios. The pottery phase dates between 1225 B.C. and 1175 B.C. Cf., A. Furumark, "Philistine Ware," in *The Chronology of Mycenaean Pottery* (Chicago: University of Chicago Press, 1941) pp. 118-21; and also Albright, *The Archaeology of Palestine*, pp. 114-15.

that it was made locally in Palestine, from memory as an imitation of what they had used at home. This helps verify the origin of the Philistines in the Aegean islands and probably, ultimately with the Pelasgians. Albright feels that the identification of "Philistine" being identical with "Pelasgian" by Bérard and Georgier (1950-51) confirms this matter.[170] He then goes a step further to note that the probable decipherment of Mycenaean Linear B script on tablets at Cnossos in Crete and at Pylus and Mycenae in Greece will eventually lead to the finding of Philistine tablets and script. Now the excavations of Franken at Tell Dier ʿAllā may have turned up some evidence for such a script.[171]

The evidence for associating this "Philistine" ware with the actual Philistines is very substantial. The pottery appears suddenly at the end of the Late Bronze Age on the Maritime coast but later farther inland. It corresponds favorably with the area occupied by the Philistines and also with finds off the Philistine coast south of Joppa.[172] Kenyon points to the clear break between the Late Bronze Age and Early Iron Age at Ashkelon where an ash layer fifty centimeters thick separates the Canaanite city from the Philistine one.[173] It is most probable, then, that the ash level represents the destruction of the old city by the Philistines when they conquered it.

Another factor to be considered is that with the appearance of the Philistine pottery the Cypriot and Mycenaean imports ceased. This would seem to indicate that the Philistines (or some branch of the "Sea Peoples") were responsible for importing the earlier originals. When they moved into the area in mass proportions it was no longer necessary to import

---

170 *Ibid.*, pp. 184-85.

171 Cf., H. J. Franken, *Excavations at Tell Deir ʿAllā* (Leiden: Brill, 1969), pp. 7 ff.

172 Cf., D. Barag, "A Survey of Pottery Rescued from the Sea off the Coast of Israel," *IEJ*, xiii (1963), pp. 13-19. He shows that Philistine pottery was found in abundance only near the area occupied by the Philistine people.

173 Kenyon, *op. cit.*, pp. 224-25.

pottery since they began making their own in Palestine. If the Philistines were not responsible for these earlier imports why did they cease such importing when they arrived in Palestine? Would not the exporters in Cyprus and Greece have continued trading the pottery in Palestine, especially with Aegean peoples living there, who would have certainly appreciated it? Since this was not the case, perhaps it indicates that early "Philistines" were moving from their Aegean homeland to Crete and Cyprus and sending local pottery on ahead in temporary trading contracts with the Near East. This again could account for a limited number of "Philistines" in Palestine at this early time to handle the trading contacts. Later the main group moved to the Palestinian coast (see map in Chapter 1). Soon the imports ceased and they began manufacturing their own pottery from memory of what they had been using.

The Mycenaeans replaced the Minoans as traders to Egypt and the Near East during the fifteenth century B.C. Stubbings notes that a number of Aegeans appear on the tombs of the officials of the Early Eighteenth Dynasty (1570-1300) in Egypt.[174] When they conquered the Minoan center at Knossos in Crete the Linear A script was soon replaced by Linear B. Linear A which Gordon deciphered to be a Semitic dialect,[175] was used by the Minoans, while Linear B was recognized by Ventris as Mycenaean Greek.[176] Yamauchi has shown that this supports Homer's statements of contact between the Greeks and Phoenicians, which the critics generally deny.[177] This contact also reached Palestine. "Canaan-

---

174 F. Stubbings, *The Rise of Mycenaean Civilization* (Cambridge: Cambridge University Press, 1963), pp. 9-14.

175 Cf., C. Gordon, "Notes on Minoan Linear A," *Antiquity,* xxxi (1957), pp. 124-30. His viewpoint, however, is still disputed.

176 Cf., M. Ventris and J. Chadwick, *Documents in Mycenaean Greek* (Cambridge: Cambridge University Press, 1956).

177 E. Yamauchi, *Greece and Babylon: Early Contacts Between the Aegean and the Near East* (Grand Rapids: Baker, 1967), pp. 33-34. This excellent work

ite" jars which had been used to export spices to Greece have been found at Mycenae. They were used in Egypt for wine storage.[178]

Mycenaean colonies spread to Crete, Cyprus, and Cilicia (northern Syria). The colony on Cyprus began to produce its own Mycenaean ware (III B) and began exporting it into Palestine. This ware has been found at Megiddo, Gezer, Beth-shemesh, Gath, Lachish, Tell elʾAjjul, and Tell Fara.

Mycenaean pottery from Tell el-Ajjul in Palestine

Mycenaean vases from Beth-shemesh in Palestine

---

covers the entire realm of Greek-Semitic contacts. His section touching on the Philistines is pp. 33-46.

178 V. Grace, "The Canaanite Jar," in S. Weinberg (ed.), *The Aegean and the Near East* (Locust Valley, New York: Augustin, 1956), pp. 80-109.

Philistine crater from Beth-shemesh

Both Mycenaean III B and III C pottery are similar to "Philistine" pottery. The main types are craters (two-handled bowls) and jugs and are buff in color with a creamy grey wash put on after baking and, then, painted in red and black designs. The craters have two tilted horizontal loop-handles for carrying and the jugs generally have a strainer spout used for straining out the barley husks from the beer. Albright concludes that the extensive production of such wine craters and beer jugs shows the Philistines were "mighty carousers."[179]

There can be no doubt of extensive trade contacts between the Aegean and the Near East long before the arrival of the Philistines in the Levant. That early Minoans and Mycenaeans could have been called "Philistines" in the Old Testament

179 Albright, *Archaeology of Palestine,* p. 115.

seems very possible from the available evidence. The assertion that the reference to the "Philistines" in the Pentateuch is an obvious anachronism need no longer be so obvious since proto-Greek peoples were trading in Palestine from the time of Abraham onwards.

Late Mycenaean III B crater from Enkomi, Cyprus (1300-1200 B.C.) similar to Philistine craters

IV

The Philistines in the Bible

The arrival of the Philistines to the shores of Palestine and the commercial contacts between the Aegean and the Near East marked an important step in the early development of the nation of Israel. Though their culture and military technology were far superior to that of Israel, the Philistines were never able to penetrate successfully the Judean hill country. They remained basically confined to the coastal plain.

THE PENTATEUCH

The first appearance of the "Philistines" in the Old Testament is in the much disputed passages of Genesis, where they have contact with Abraham and Isaac. Sometime after the destruction of Sodom and Gomorrah, Abraham moved from the plain to the Negeb ("the south country") and it was here that Albright believes he became involved in the donkey caravan trade using Gerar as his base of operation.[1] Abraham's movements from Mesopotamia to Haran to Canaan,

[1] Cf., his remarks in his "Introduction" to H. Gunkel's, *The Legends of Genesis* (New York: Shockren, 1964), pp. x-xi. He notes that there is substantial textual evidence of donkey caravaneering in the Near East as early as 2300 B.C.

then, involved moving between trading stations and caravan centers. After arriving in Canaan he apparently continued moving between such posts in Syria, Palestine, and northern Egypt, thus amassing a vast fortune.

In Genesis 20, Abraham moved south and "tented" between Kadesh and Shur and then settled in Gerar. The ancient city was important in patriarchal times and was located in the low ridge of foothills below the mountains of Judah. Archaeologists have disputed its location but Tell Abu Hureira, excavated in 1956 by Alon seems most likely to be ancient Gerar.[2] It substantiated evidence of a permanent settlement throughout every period of the Bronze and Iron Ages. Alon found numerous evidences of Philistine iron-working and iron instruments at the site.[3] Of course these came from the Iron Age period.

This passage makes no statement about Gerar or its king, Abimelech, being "Philistines," but Genesis 21 declares Abimelech was the ruler of the "land of the Philistines." Genesis 26:15 indicates that the Philistines were actually the ones in contact with Abraham. Since there is substantial evidence of contacts at this time between the Aegean peoples and Near Eastern Semites, there is no reason to throw this reference out as an unhistorical anachronism. There is evidence of early sea voyages across the Mediterranean by Syro-Phoenician sailors as early as the second millennium B.C.[4] Minoan metalurgy was in use in Egypt and Phoenicia as early

---

[2] Cf., the report by Y. Aharoni, "The Land of Gerar," *Israel Exploration Journal,* vi (1956), pp. 26-32. This identification is also accepted by F. Cross and G. E. Wright, *JBL,* lxxv (1956), pp. 212-13; J. Finegan, *Light from the Ancient Past* (Princeton University Press, 1959), p. 146; and T. C. Mitchell, *NBD,* p. 463. For the earlier identification of the site of Tell Jemmeh as Gerar, see W. F. Petrie, *Gerar,* (London: British School of Archaeology in Egypt, 1928).

[3] Aharoni, *op. cit.*

[4] Cf., G. Dossin, *"Les archives èconomiques du palis de mari,"* *Syria,* xx (1939), pp. 105-26.

as the third millennium B.C.![5] Thus, contacts between East and West were moving in both directions as Astour has so thoroughly shown.[6] Both Minoan and Mycenaean pottery and art have been found in abundance in Palestine long before the mass migration of the "Philistines" there in 1200 B.C.[7] Other evidence of early Aegean peoples active in Palestine are the anthropoid clay coffins found in Palestine, Egypt, and Nubia in relation to Philistine mercenaries stationed these locations. The burial customs reflect Aegean practices (e.g., the gold foil mouth plates on the corpses) and contain Mycenaean pottery, indicating that they predate the production of Philistine ware.[8] Add to these factors the evidence pointed out by Wright that the Hebrew word *p^eli̇̌štîm* was used for all the "Sea Peoples" without discrimination.[9]

Thus it is certainly not unlikely that Abraham could have had a commercial contact with an outpost of Aegean peoples trading in Gerar. Again it is not unlikely that they could have been identified as *p^eli̇̌štîm* by a later copiest of the Book of Genesis. It may even be that they were actual "proto-Philistines." As has been shown in the previous chapter, there was a trading route between Crete (*kap-ta-ra* of the Mari docu-

---

[5] G. V. Childe points this out in *New Light on the Most Ancient East* (New York: Grove Press, 1957), pp. 157 and 177.

[6] M. Astour, *Hellenosemitica* (Leiden: Brill, 1967); this valuable work should be thoroughly consulted regarding Aegean and Near Eastern relationships.

[7] Cf., above throughout chapter 3. Also note the comments of J. Pendlebury, *The Archaeology of Crete, an Introduction* (London: Burns & Oats, 1939) p. 170; W. F. Albright, "Some Oriental Glosses on the Homeric Problem," *American Journal of Archaeology,* liv (1950), pp. 162-76; F. Stubbings, *Mycenaean Pottery in the Levant* (Cambridge: Cambridge University Press, 1951), pp. 84-86; W. A. Heurtley, "The Relationship between 'Philistine' and Mycenaean Pottery," *QDAP,* v (1936), pp. 90-110 (including illustrated comparisons).

[8] See the remarks by G. E. Wright, "Philistine Coffins and Mercenaries," *Biblical Archaeologist,* xxii (1959), pp. 54-66. He points out that the clay coffins from Tomb 570 at Lachish are the oldest, even though in Palestine, and must pre-date even the arrival of the Israelites to Palestine!

[9] *Ibid.,* p. 59, n. 10.

ments) and Mesopotamia via north Syria and Palestine.[10] Through this commerce Mycenaean pottery was brought into the Near East at an early time. It is possible that early "Philistines" living temporarily in Crete could have been agents of this trade. J.L. Swauger of the Carnegie Museum and Director of the Ashdod Excavation has recently suggested that this pottery was brought to Palestine via Cyprus by the first groups of Sea Peoples to settle there.[11] When the Philistines later moved to the coastal plain of Palestine the imports began to diminish implying that perhaps they had been the merchants of this ware before moving.

From a strictly archaeological standpoint the whole question must be left open since there is no actual "Philistine" evidence at Gerar from patriarchal times. On the other hand, there is ample evidence of Aegean peoples trading in the Near East at that time.

In Genesis 20, Abraham journeyed to Gerar where he met and feared Abimelech ("my-father-is-king"). His spontaneous reaction toward self-preservation led to the old lie that Sarah, his wife, was his sister. Thus, he protected himself from the possibility of Abimelech killing him in order to take Sarah. However, he was not able thereby to protect Sarah at all and Abimelech took her into his harem. The name "Abi-melech" is undoubtedly Semitic, though, it was probably a title rather than a personal name.[12] Thus, Isaac, years later, meets "Abimelech" at Gerar, but the two are not necessarily the same person. Though this story is similar to the one involving pharaoh of Egypt in Genesis 12, the two are not necessarily duplicates. Notice that Abraham states (v. 13) that he made

---

[10] Cf., Dossin, *op. cit.*

[11] J. L. Swauger, "Fifth Season at Tell Ashdod," *ASOR Newsletter,* No. 5, Jan. 1970. The results of the 1969 finds yet await publication.

[12] Cf., Astour, op. cit., pp. 126-27. D. Kidner, *Genesis: an Introduction and Commentary* (Tyndale Series) (London: Tyndale Press, 1967), p. 138, agrees that the name is a royal title. Note that Gideon's son, king of Shechem, took this title also (Judg. 8:31).

this precaution his normal policy in the face of possible death. There are also substantial points of difference between the two accounts: the two different places (Egypt and Philistia); two different monarchs (one idolatrous, the other fearing God); different circumstances (famine and a nomadic migration); and very different conclusions (first, rejection from Egypt and, secondly, an invitation to stay in Philistia).[13]

Speiser, however, holds this up as an example of duplication of the same original story by the later editors "J" and "E."[14] In contrast to this Cassuto of the Hebrew University shows that the name *ʾElōhīm* is always used in Genesis in relation to alien people or when God manifests Himself to Gentiles (i.e., Abimelech). He is convinced that the variations in the use of the names *Yhwh* and *ʾElōhīm* can always be explained on this basis.[15] Therefore, the use of these names depends upon context rather than the so-called editors of the Pentateuch. Though Abimelech feared God he was not a member of the covenant who knew that *ʾElōhīm* as *Yhwh* (Yahweh).

God speaks directly to Abimelech to warn him of his serious action against Abraham's wife. He informs the king that He expects him to honor the sanctity of the marriage bond. Abraham had sinned through unbelief and now Abimelech had acted in ignorance of Sarah's status.[16] The reason

---

13 These and other points are made by H. Leupold, *Exposition of Genesis* (Columbus: Wartburg Press, 1942), pp. 579-80.

14 E. A. Speiser, *The Anchor Bible: Genesis* (Garden City, New York: Doubleday, 1964), p. 151. He feels that the story of Isaac is original to "E" with the anachronistic insertion of "Philistine" being made by "J" (p. 159).

15 Cf., his excellent comments in U. Cassuto, *The Documentary Hypothesis and the Composition of the Pentateuch.* Trans. I. Abrahams (Jerusalem: Magnes Press, 1961), pp. 40-41. His survey on the use of the divine names in the Pentateuch (pp. 15-41) shows that *Yhwh* is always used in relation with God's people, Israel, while *ʾElōhīm* is only used with alien peoples (cf., also pp. 60-61).

16 J. Calvin, *A Commentary on Genesis,* Trans. J. King (London: Banner of Truth, 1965 reprint of 1847 trans.), p. 524, presents the view that what Abim-

for Abimelech's interest in Sarah was probably for the purpose of a marriage alliance with Abraham since she was now ninety years old (Gen. 17:17).[17] If Abimelech were the chieftain of a group of minority Aegean peoples involved in commerce in Palestine an alliance with this powerful and wealthy nomad, Abraham, would have been very desirable. Thus, his lavish gifts (vv. 14-18) showed his desire to gain Abraham's support and friendship. That Abraham was a wealthy, nomadic merchant is well attested from Scripture as well as from contemporary culture of that day. Cyrus Gordon writes:

> Abraham comes from beyond the Euphrates, plies his trade in Canaan, visits Egypt, deals with Hittites, makes treaties with Philistines, forms military alliances with Amorites, fights kinglets from as far off as Elam, marries the Egyptian Hagar, etc. His contacts and freedom of movement reflect a sophisticated milieu where an international order . . . made such a career and such enterprise possible.[18]

It is also interesting that Gordon mentions Abraham's contact with the Philistines without critical comments. The same political and commercial advantages enjoyed by Abraham could have also benefited other foreign peoples in the land. Later the situation changed enough so that even Abraham's descendents felt compelled to move. It is possible that these early Aegean people at Gerar did the same, thus leaving little material evidence of their stay.

Having explained his "half-truth" to Abimelech, Abraham

---

elech was ignorant of was the severe penalty for his action. However, it seems that he was mainly ignorant of what wrong he had done.

[17] Cf., Kidner, *op. cit.*, p. 138 and Leupold, *op. cit.*, p. 583.

[18] C. H. Gordon, "Abraham and the Merchants of Ura," *Journal of Near Eastern Studies,* xvii (1959), p. 30. He suggests that Abraham was originally a merchant trader from the city of Ura in Northern Mesopotamia. Cf., also a reference to this by C. Pfeiffer who accepts this evidence in *The Patriarchal Age* (Grand Rapids: Baker, 1961), p. 71.

announced that his half-sister, Sarah was also his wife (v. 12). Abimelech then invited Abraham to remain in his domain (v. 15) and Abraham took him up on it (21:34). However, trouble soon arose between their servants. This incident is recorded in Genesis 21:22-34, at Beer-sheba on the outskirts of Abimelech's realm. Kidner states that this scene is about twenty-five miles from Gerar, where disputes could easily arise over pasturing rights.[19] This time Phicol, the "chief captain of the host," appears with Abimelech. His name is definitely non-Semitic. Bright suggests that it is Hurrian and Astour shows that it is probably a title, rather than a personal name.[20] This could account for Isaac meeting persons named Abimelech and Phicol at Gerar, since they would not necessarily have to be the same persons with whom Abraham dealt. Speiser admits that he does not know what to do with *Pî-kôl* in this passage and wants to change his name to Abimelech also![21] Kidner also suggests the names may be recurring family names.[22]

Another factor to consider is the use of the Hebrew verb with the *waw* conversive, indicating that "as often as Abraham took Abimelech to task about the wells . . . he would answer . . ." Abraham evidently had to make his complaint several times so that a running rivalry over the wells makes the reopening of the situation with Isaac all the more likely.[23]

---

19 *Op. cit.*, p. 141.

20 J. Bright, *A History of Israel* (Philadelphia: Westminster, 1959), pp. 73-74; M. Astour, *op. cit.*, pp. 126-27.

21 *Op. cit.*, p. 201.

22 *Op. cit.*, p. 154. Cf., also K. A. Kitchen, *Ancient Orient and Old Testament* (Chicago: Inter-Varsity, 1966), pp. 80-81. He points to the practice in Egypt of naming sons after grandfathers ("papponymy"). This pattern was used for as many as four consecutive generations (e.g. Ammenemes I–Khnumhotep I–Ammenemes II–Khnumhotep II). He points out that no one would claim these as literary doublets as is done with the references to Abimelech and Phicol. Cf., also G. Posener, *Littérature et Politique dans l 'Egypt de la XIIe dynastie* (Paris: Champion, 1956), pp. 50 ff.

23 This suggestion is the observation of Kidner, *op. cit.*, p. 141. Leupold, *op.*

Abimelech wanted to initiate a covenant with Abraham and Abraham was agreeable except in regard to the matter of settling the well dispute, which seems to have been going on for some time. Abimelech, however, claimed to have been unaware of it and promised to rectify the matter. The subsequent gift of sheep and oxen to Abimelech shows Abraham's desire to correct the situation and seal a covenant with Abimelech. It is most likely that these animals were slain to seal the covenant in blood. Possibly Abraham and Abimelech passed between their divided parts to substantiate the covenant. Nevertheless, Abraham also gave seven ewe lambs to Abimelech as a goodwill gift and in accepting them, Abimelech committed himself to Abraham's terms and recognized the well as Abraham's rightful possession.

According to this incident the place was named "Beersheba" for the giving of the seven lambs as well as for the oath. Both words: "seven" and "swear" have the same root and, thus, there appears to be a play on words here. However, *šabhaʿ* is never used in place of *šebhuʿah* ("oath"). Thus "well of seven" seems more correct than "well of oath."[24] The paronomasia remains but it is not really clear as to the original meaning. Following this incident Abraham is said to have planted a tamarisk tree[25] here (v. 33) and called on Yahweh by the name *elʿôlām* ("the everlasting God"). Some have used this incident to say that Abraham was following a Canaanite practice of worshiping a deity who lived in the trees.[26] However, there is no indication of this in the text.

cit., pp. 611-12 argues against this on the basis of E. Koenig's view in *Lehrgebaeude der Hebraeischen Sprache,* Part II. (Leizig: Hinrichs, 1897), p. 3701. However, most recent commentators agree that it does imply consecutive action as Leupold admits.

[24] Cf., Leupold, *op. cit.,* p. 613, Kidner, *op. cit.,* p. 142. For a contrary position see Calvin, *op. cit.,* p. 556.

[25] This passage should read a "tree" not a "grove of trees" (A.V.). The root parables the Arabic "tamarisk." Such a tree was a fitting memorial to God for His blessings to Abraham.

[26] Cf., Speiser, *op. cit.,* p. 159. Another misrepresentation of this passage is to

The verbs imply he planted the tree immediately and worshiped. It would have taken years for the tree to grow enough to be called the "tree of a god."

Being convinced that he should remain in the southern end of the "promised land" Abraham remained many days in the "land of the Philistines." Though Abimelech and Phicol could easily have been Aegean peoples of a proto-Philistine type, it is highly unlikely that the coastal area was called "the land of the Philistines" in Abraham's time. This, however, is probably a later insertion in the text by a copiest to identify the location. It does not necessarily prove that the whole story is to be doubted.

The final Philistine contact comes in Genesis 26, where Isaac also journeys to Gerar at the time of a famine. This famine is distinguished in the text from the earlier one in Abraham's time, the one described in Genesis 12. Thus, Isaac too seeks refuge in the "Philistine" city of Gerar, where he encounters Abimelech and Phicol several years after Abraham had been there. Since their "names" may also be "titles" it is possible that these were two different people from those Abraham encountered.[27]

When the men of Gerar showed some interest in his wife, Isaac followed his father's weakness of lying about her being his "sister." However, in this account no attempt was made to take his wife, as happened to Sarah, and they lived there "a long time" before they were found out by the king. Eventually, he observed Isaac "caressing" Rebekah ("fondling," RSV; "sporting," AV) and concluded that she must be

---

eliminate all the personal elements as legendary. Cf., H. Gunkel, *The Legends of Genesis* (New York: Shocken Books, 1964 reprint of 1901 trans.), p. 20. He sees Abraham-Isaac and Abimelech as legendary characters representing a personification of an original dispute over wells between the people of Gerar and the neighboring Bedouins. However, even Albright who wrote the introduction to this edition says the stories of the patriarchs are much more historical than Gunkel admits and that his mistakes were inevitable because of his lack of current information (pp. x-xi).

27 Cf., comments above, note 20, note 22.

his wife and not his sister. Although Isaac was rebuked by the pagan king he was, nevertheless, allowed to remain in the area and was blessed of God despite his lapse of faithfulness: "and the man became great, and went forward, and grew until he became very great" (v. 13). Isaac soon found success in farming as well as accumulating flocks, herds and servants, so that the "Philistines" both envied and feared him. This fact is more easily explainable if the Philistines were a foreign minority group engaged in commerce in Canaan than if they were native Canaanites.

In the meantime the old well controversy was renewed. Abimelech eventually requested Isaac to leave Gerar (v. 16) which left him trapped between the hostile city and a waterless countryside, for the Philestines had earlier filled in Abraham's wells.[28] Isaac then tented in the valley below Gerar and began to re-dig the wells. His excavations again placed him in a place of power and prominence and Abimelech came to him with Ahuzzath and Phicol to make a treaty with him (v. 26).[29] The covenant revived the earlier one with Abraham which was definitely in need of renewal. A feast was then prepared as a sign of good will in keeping the covenant. The "Philistine" diplomats remained over night and returned the next day. As the scene of Genesis begins to shift to Jacob the Philistines disappear from the picture and little is known of what transpired on the coast in the following years.

In the rest of the Pentateuch there are only two references to the "Philistines" and both are in the Book of Exodus and come at the time of the Hebrews' exodus from Egypt. In Exodus 13:17 we are told that God led the people of Israel through the wilderness of the Red Sea rather than the more direct route through the "land of the Philistines." The reason given is that God did not want them to turn back in the face

[28] This is Kidner's observation, *op. cit.*, p. 154.

[29] The name Ahuzzath has the *aṯ* ending as "Goliath" and appears similar to forms found in names of western Anatolia. Cf., Mitchell, *AOTS*, p. 415.

of war. The other reference appears in Exodus 23:31, where God promises the Israelites that they will conquer Canaan "by little and little" (piece by piece) and their boundaries shall extend from the Red Sea to the sea of the Philistines. This passage is important in that it specifies that the total conquest would be a slow process. Thus, the lightning conquest under Joshua gained only temporary control of the land and the Book of Judges testifies to the long and tedious task involved in bringing Canaan under final control. The Philistines were the most troublesome of all to the Israelites and they retained control of the coastal plain until the time of David. The reference to the "sea of the Philistines" must be to the Great Sea (Mediterranean).

There are numerous problems involved in these references, though at first glance they might seem minor. One relates to the date of the Exodus. Those maintaining that the Exodus was in the time of Ramses rather than c. 1450 B.C. could point to this reference to show that the Philistines were already in Canaan at the time of Ramses. However, there is ample evidence to show the penetration of Aegean peoples into Palestine in the fifteenth century B.C. so that a later copiest could have identified the coastal area as the "land of the Philistines." That war was going on there is certain for the Canaanite kings were at war with one another, as well as being in conflict with Egyptian armies that contained Aegean mercenaries and possibly early "Philistines."[30]

It would have taken time for these early Philistines to make contact with Palestine and migrate far enough into the

[30] Cf., above chapter under sub-title: "Archaeology and Philistine Migrations." The Phaistos disc of the Middle Minoan III period (c. 1600 B.C.) contains hieroglyphic-like syllabaries of which one is a man with a feathered helmet or headdress. The symbol looks exactly like pictures of Philistines in Egyptian carvings. Cf., comments of R. A. S. Macalister, *The Philistines; Their History and Civilization* (Schweich Lectures, 1911). (London: British Academy, 1913), pp. 83-86; J. Pendlebury, *The Archaeology of Crete, an Introduction* (London: Burns & Oats, 1939), p. 170. The Minoans had ample contact with Palestine and early Pelasgoi (proto-Philistines) could have been among them.

The Phaestos Disc (Face II)

Near East to become Egyptian mercenaries in the mid-thirteenth century. For when the great mass of Sea Peoples came into Palestine in c. 1200 B.C., some "Philistines" were already there to unite with them against the Egyptians, and others were serving the Egyptians as their mercenaries.[31] Thus it is not impossible that the route up the coast was at times touched by the Sea Peoples. Mainly, though, the Egyptian garrisons were there and would have fought the Hebrew people. In God's plan they were to enter the land by a more indirect route through the back door of the Jordan.

---

[31] See especially the observations of G. E. Wright, "Philistine Coffins and Mercenaries," *Biblical Archaeologist*, xxii (1959), pp. 54-66.

JOSHUA

In the Book of Joshua the "Philistines" are mentioned only once (13:2, 3). They do not appear as an active group in the text of Joshua but they are listed as a part of the unconquered territory. Verse two reads: "This is the land that yet remains: all the borders of the Philistines, and all Geshuri." At this time (c. 1400 B.C.) the initial conquest was over but the coastal area remained out of Israel's control. Since the Philistines are not active in the Book of Joshua and are not listed among the inhabitants of the land (12:8), they were probably still confined to the coastal area of the Negeb (Exod. 13:17) engaged in trade in the same area where they appear in the patriarchal narratives (Gen. 21:32; 27:1). Notice that the five cities of the later Philistines are listed in verse three as being "Canaanite" in Joshua's time. Davis notes thag according to Joshua 11:22, the Anakim were inhabiting Gaza, Gath, and Ashdod at that time.[32] Thus the cities later under the five lords of the Philistines were at this time controlled by the Canaanites through their "cousins" the Anakim. Rea has suggested that in light of this, verse three is probably an early scribal notation that the domain of the five lords of the Philistines still belonged to the Canaanites in Joshua's day, while the Aegean merchants were still confined in limited numbers to the south.[33]

JUDGES

The major importance of the Philistines to the early his-

[32] J. J. Davis, *Conquest and Crisis* (Grand Rapids: Baker, 1969), p. 78. Also many believe the later Philistines to have included some remnant of the Anakim among them (e.g., Goliath). Cf., G. H. Gordon, "The Role of the Philistines," *Antiquity,* xxx (1956), pp. 22-26, and E. MacLaurin," Anak/*Avae" Vetus Testamentum,* xv (1965), pp. 468-74.

[33] J. Rea, "Joshua," in C. Pfeiffer and E. Harrison (eds.), *The Wycliffe Bible Commentary* (Chicago: Moody Press, 1963), p. 222. His opinion is followed by Davis, *op. cit.,* p. 78.

tory of Israel appears in the Book of Judges and that of I Samuel. The Philistines dominate this period as one of Israel's most prominent enemies. By this time the great migration of Sea Peoples to the Near East had been completed and the Philistines appear in full possession of the maritime coast of Palestine.

Early in the period of the judges (c. 1250 B.C.), however, the Philistines were just coming into Palestine. Perhaps they were on their way to an eventual clash with the Egyptians.[34] Bands of Philistines and Thekels began raiding the mouth of the delta and later came in a great horde attempting to conquer Egypt. It was probably during the early period of their initial mass migrations that they appear in Judges 3:31 in conflict with Shamgar.

1. Shamgar Ben Anath

In Judges 3:3 God stated that He allowed certain people to remain in the land to prove Israel's faithfulness to Him. Among these were the Philistines from whom they would learn war. The passage mentions the five lords of the Philistines. The Hebrew word "lord" (*seren*) is thought to be a Philistine loan-word for it is generally used only in connection with references to the Philistines.[35]

As these new Philistine invaders entered the land they posed a threat to the Israelite people and it probably is within this context that Shamgar confronted them. The Philistines were not yet permanently settled in Palestine and their attempted invasion of Egypt was yet to come. Shamgar appears on the scene to slay six hundred Philistines with an ox goad and "he also delivered Israel." Nothing more is said of him and the reference might easily be taken as an editor's

---

[34] J. Garstang felt they began to arrive at this time during the reign of Ramses II. Cf., *Joshua-Judges* (London: Constable & Co., 1931) pp. 88 ff.

[35] Cf., Davis, *op. cit.*, pp. 78-81.

addition except that he is also mentioned in Deborah's song in Judges 5:6.

Deborah says of Shamgar and Jael,[36] that in their day the highways of Israel were unoccupied and people had to travel the lesser byways. Cundall suggests reading "highways" as "caravans," noting that commercial trade by caravan ceased at that time because of the dangers of being on the open highways that were controlled by the enemies of Israel.[37]

In Judges 3:31 the characteristic features of the narration are absent. Israel's sin that leads to judgment is not mentioned, and there is no reference to a Philistine oppression of any specified duration. It is likely then that no Philistine "oppression," therefore, is involved: but only a rising menace to the people of Israel. Therefore, it is possible that Shamgar was not really a "judge," since Ehud was the major "judge" of that time. It should be observed that he is mentioned in connection with the woman Jael who was not a judge but somewhat of a local "hero."

Many commentators look on Shamgar as an insertion by a later redactor.[38] They see it as an addition to the so-called "Deuteronomic" framework of the history of the judges. The editor of the Book of Judges is seen as an historian writing during the Assyrian period in Israel of the events back in the time of the judges.[39] Kaufmann strongly attacked this concept of interpreting Biblical history, saying the Book of

---

36 The woman who "nailed" Sisera, the Canaanite army captain, to the floor of her tent with a tent peg and hammer.

37 Cf., A. E. Cundall, *Judges: An Introduction and Commentary* (Tyndale Series). (London: Tyndale Press, 1968), p. 95. This is the most recent and one of the finest evangelical commentaries on the Book of Judges available.

38 Cf., in this regard the comments of J. MacKenzie, *The World of the Judges* (Englewood Cliffs, New Jersey: Prentice-Hall, 1966), pp. 125-26. He believes the Shamgar incident was inserted at this point within the original story to give a reason for the reference to him in the "Song of Deborah" (ch. 5).

39 For a discussion of "Deuteronomic" history in modern theory see M. Burrows, "Ancient Israel," in R. Dentan (ed.), *The Idea of History in the Ancient Near East* (New Haven: Yale University Press, 1955), pp. 117-21.

Judges and the other early historical books have not undergone a Deuteronomistic redaction and heaps up his evidence to show that the antiquity of the historicity of Judges proves that its narrative material is extremely ancient.[40] Cundall asks the pointed question: "surely a redactor inserting an extra character into the book would take care to conform to the pattern of the book?"[41] Otherwise, the name would really seem out of place as "Shamgar" does here. It is the omissions, however, in relation to the Shamgar incident that are most important. He probably was not an actual judge but rather a local hero of some sort who between the time of Ehud and Deborah battled the Philistines and thus "delivered" Israel from potential danger.

The name "Shamgar" is definitely not Hebrew and seems to be of Hittite or Hurrian origin.[42] He may have been a Canaanite himself or of mixed Israelite background. He is introduced as a hero. He is also called "son of Anath" which may be a reference to the Canaanite goddess of sex and war named Anath and related to Baal worship. Garstang suggested thag Shamgar Ben Anath in this passage was the Ben Anath of Galilee, a Syrian sea captain with whom Ramses II had a royal alliance by which Egypt may have protected Palestine from early Philistine aggression.[43] However, Anath sanctuaries were common among the Canaanites of this time and the name likewise was a common name.

One should also notice that Shamgar's weapon was an ox goad, hardly the weapon of a sea captain! It was a long-handled, pointed stick tipped with metal and used to prod

---

40 Y. Kaufmann, *The Biblical Account of the Conquest of Palestine* (Jerusalem: Magnes Press, 1953), pp. 4-7; 63-64. He shows that Judges 2-3 presents a very unfavorable and unidealistic picture of Israel's history during the early period of the Judges and is not "true" to the Deuteronomistic viewpoint at all!

41 *Op. cit.*, p. 80.

42 *Cf., MacKenzie, op. cit.*, p. 125, and Cundall, *op. cit.*, p. 80.

43 J. Garstang, *op. cit.*, p. 287-88. His comments bear more consideration than usually given though they may not be correct.

animals. Its size (c. ten feet) and point made it a ready weapon to use in an emergency. The Philistines later became famous for disarming their enemies and it could be that Shamgar had no other weapon available to him. He slew six hundred men with it. This may represent either a single combat total or a lifetime total. Because the Philistines were the enemies of Israel he was looked upon as a deliverer. Whoever he really was may never be determined but he is essential to the narrative because he is referred to again in Deborah's song, indicating that she knew of his exploits. Despite his unknown background and humble weapon, he was used of God to spare His people Israel.

2. Samson

The Philistines do not play a major part in the book until the Samson stories in Judges 13-16. In the meanwhile they had been repelled by Ramses III of Egypt and settled on the Palestinian coast, while Israel held the mountain area. They established "lords" in their five-city-pentapolis and began to push eastward into the Shephelah border and the foothills of Judah. At this point they again came into direct conflict with Israel and Samson was raised up by God to "begin to deliver" Israel from the Philistines.

a) Oppression under the Philistines (Judg. 13:1)

Judges 13 introduces one to the Samson narratives with the statement that the children of Israel "did evil again in the sight of the Lord," which resulted in His delivering them into the hands of the Philistines for forty years. This lasted until the victories of Samuel and David over these enemies of Israel. These Aegean people were far superior to the Hebrews and Canaanites in culture and military craft. Their city-state government ruled over by the five "lords" of the pentapolis was a strong centralized power against the loosely organized tribal government of the Hebrews. The Philistine monopoly on the use of iron also kept the Israelites in subjection (I Sam. 13:19-22). The Israelites were not permitted to make iron swords or spears and Saul's army is said to have been devoid of such weapons. Therefore, it is not unlikely that during this period the Israelite warriors used such strange weapons: Shamgar's ox goad, Samson's jaw bone, and David's sling.

Despite the Philistines' prowess, they soon amalgamated their religious practices with those of the Canaanites whom they conquered on the coast. The religio-cultural diffusion that followed enabled the Philistines to adjust to their Semitic surroundings while still retaining much of their Aegean background. By the time of Samson (early eleventh century B.C.) this process was well established and the military confederacy was also in process. Gaza, Ashkelon, and Ashdod were old Canaanite cities on the coast while Gath and Ekron were further inland on the western edge of the Shephelah. Gath was also formerly a Canaanite city, whereas, Ekron appears to have been founded by the Philistines themselves.[44]

b) Birth of Samson (Judg. 13:2-25)

Samson was born to the family of Manoah of the city of Zorah and of the tribe of Dan (Judg. 13:2). The Hebrew name "Samson" (*šimšon*) seems to be derived from the word for "sun" (*šemeš*). This is also supported by the fact that Zorah was opposite the town of Beth-shemesh ("house of the sun").[45] The name was probably originally Canaanite for it

[44] This conclusion is made by Y. Aharoni and M. Avi-Yonah, *The Macmillan Bible Atlas* (New York: Macmillan, 1968), p. 56.

[45] Cf., Ezra 4:8 where Shimshai is pronounced Samsai. P. Cassel, *The Book of Judges* in J. Lange (ed.), *Commentary on the Holy Scriptures* (trans. P. Schaff). (Grand Rapids: Zondervan, n.d., reprint of 1871 ed.), p. 191, mentions that the derivation of "Samson" from *šēmēš* is of long standing among Jewish expositors. He criticizes Keil and Delitzsch for following Josephus in trying to derive the name from the root *šameš* ("be strong or daring").

occurs in the Ugaritic texts of the fourteenth and fifteenth centuries B.C.

Samson's hometown of Zorah was a small border town in the eastern Shephelah on the border between Dan and Judah. However, it was also on the ever-shifting border between Israel and Philistia and brought Samson into early contacts with his people's enemies. It lay on the northern rim overlooking the Valley of Sorek which was later the scene of most of Samson's exploits. Immediately opposite the valley was the town of Beth-shemesh which was under strong Philistine influence.[46] In this region of the Valley of Sorek Samson spent the major part of his life. His recorded exploits

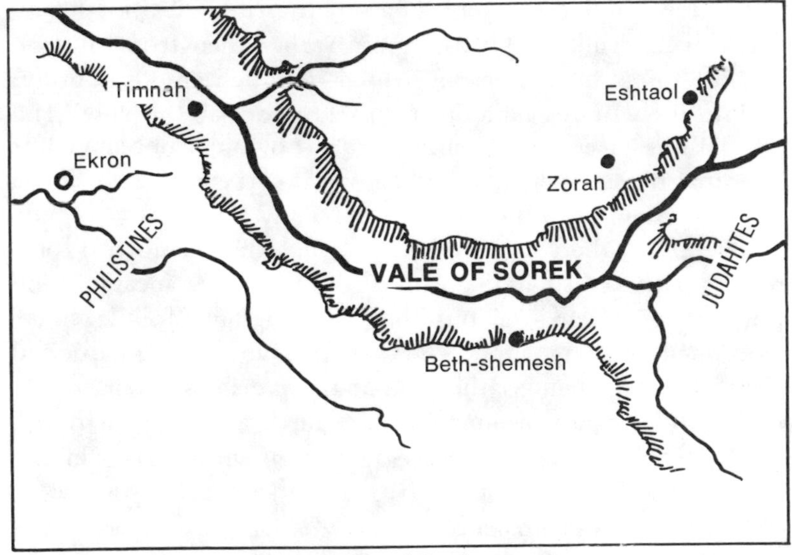

Valley of Sorek

46 The excavations there in 1928-32 directed by Elihu Grant showed an abundance of Philistine pottery and objects indicating their incursion inland. The city later was apparently recaptured by the Israelites (cf., Josh. 21:16). In I Samuel 6, the Philistines returned the unwanted ark of the covenant there, implying that it was then in Israelite hands. Cf., Grant's report in *Beth-shemesh* (Haverford: Haverford Archaeological Expedition, 1929). Also see above "Beth-shemesh" in ch. 3.

generally place him between Zorah on the high ridge and the Philistine town of Timnah (or Timnath) down the valley. The tribe of Dan had unsuccessfully attempted to settle this area and probably had migrated northward by Samson's time (Judg. 18). Thus, Samson would have been one of the remnants of the Danites still in the Shephelah area.[47]

The angel of the Lord appeared to Samson's parents and announced his birth in a formula similar to that found in Isaiah 7:14.[48] The angel explained that the promised son was to become a "Nazirite" unto God from birth.[49] The stipulations of the vow found in Numbers 6 are paralleled in the restrictions placed upon Samson's mother in Judges 13:4-5. The three stipulations were: (1) not to drink wine nor strong drink (i.e., drink made from grain rather than from grapes), (2) not to eat any "unclean" thing or touch any dead body, (3) not to cut his hair during the period of the vow. The restrictions given to the mother are obviously intended for the time of her pregnancy while she is carrying the child and afterwards apply to the child himself.[50]

Therefore, the Nazirite vow becomes the theological focal point to the story of Samson and gives it its meaning and purpose. MacKenzie claims that the original "folk-legends" contained nothing about the Nazirite vow but mentioned only the long hair as the source of Samson's strength. He contends that the prologue of the birth announcement was added later to give the stories a "theological basis" in the

---

47 This is the conclusion of Cundall, *op. cit.*, p. 154, and seems most correct since the appendix of ch. 17-21 records a summary of events that actually occurred chronologically between ch. 2 and 3. Cf., chart in Davis, *op. cit.*, p. 97.

48 For a recent discussion of the relationship of angels' announcement formulas see E. Hindson, "Isaiah's Immanuel," *Grace Journal*, x (1969) pp. 3 ff.

49 The RSV reading "Nazirite" is to be preferred over the AV reading "Nazarite" since the term derives from the Hebrew *nāzîr*, "to be separated" or "consecrated."

50 MacKenzie, *op. cit.*, p. 151, is completely wrong when he says that the restriction against drinking applied only to the mother and not to the child!

concept of a Nazirite vow.[51] He unfortunately overlooks two important factors in the narrative. First, the strength of Samson is clearly said to lie ultimately not in the length of his hair but in the fact that he was "moved" by the spirit of Yahweh (Judg. 13:25; 14:6; 14:19; 15:14). When he lost his unusual strength the "Lord was departed from him" (Judg. 16:20). Secondly, the events of Samson's life clearly show that he broke each of the three stipulations of the Nazirite vow (Judg. 14:8-9; 14:10; 16:19). The following comments will clarify this matter. If the Nazirite concept was not original to the stories, how is it that these three elements "accidentally" appear in the so-called original contents of the narrative? Clearly the stories have no significant meaning apart from the place of the Nazirite vow.

The ordinary Nazirite vow was entered voluntarily for a temporary period and, thus, the restrictions of the vow were also temporary. However, in Samson's life the vow was neither voluntary nor temporary and placed him in a unique category of "Nazirite." The purpose of this special son was that he was to "begin to deliver" Israel from the Philistine oppression. It may appear that his was a limited task from the start but it was extremely essential to the nation of Israel because she had lapsed into the complacency of coexistence with the Philistines. She freely communicated and traded back and forth. Intermarriage was also becoming popular between the two groups and Israel would eventually have lost control of her nation as well as her national distinction as a people. The crisis was at a peak in Samson's day and the men of Israel even criticized his exploits against the Philistines: "Know you not that the Philistines are rulers over us, what is it you have done unto us?"

[51] *Ibid.* MacKenzie has many helpful comments to make on the Book of Judges and is aware of recent interpretive views as well as pertinent archaeological data. However, he seems always ready to cast each event of the Biblical record into the most radical framework possible. He appears to go out of his way to overlook the clear statements in the book itself!

At the end of chapter thirteen Samson is born, begins to grow, and is blessed by the Lord. God is involved from the beginning as having a very definite place in the events that transpire. As Samson grew he began to experience the moving of the Spirit of the Lord upon him "at times." Like the other judges he received this charismatic anointing for the task to which he was called. In Samson's case this meant the endowment of spectacular human strength to wage a one-man campaign against the Philistines. This initial activity is said to have happened in the "camp of Dan between Zorah and Eshtaol" (v. 25). The reference to Dan as a camp rather than a territory implies that this was a temporary habitation which Cundall suggests may have been a displaced person's camp.[52]

Samson's career is depicted as that of a "judge" though he is never called such until Judges 15:20, where he is said to have judged Israel for twenty years. It is difficult to determine whether this means a total "lifetime" of twenty years or twenty years after the exploits prior to chapter sixteen.[53] The word "judge" in Hebrew is *šôpēṭ* and refers to "rulers" rather than magistrates. The root is derived from the noun *mišpaṭ* ("judgment" or "justice"). It is also found in Akkadian, Phoenician, Aramaic and even Punic.[54] The basic concept has to do with the verdict given by a judge and is descriptive of every phase of the judge's work. Therefore, the noun *mišpaṭ* means the judgment given by the *šôpēṭ* and, thus, may mean justice, ordinance, or codified *tôrâ* (law) given by God.[55] Since Yahweh is the God of *mišpaṭ* (Gen.

52 *Op. cit.*, p. 160-61.

53 Cassel, *op. cit.*, p. 211, takes the latter to be the case, with Samson settling down for twenty quiet years as a judge in Hebron before his mistakes at Gaza and with Delilah.

54 Notice the cognate parallel of the Akkadian *shapitu* and the Phoenician *shuphetim*. Cf., Z. Harris, *A Grammar of the Phoenician Language* (London: 1936), p. 153. In Carthage the local magistrates were called *sufetes,* a term they probably borrowed from their contacts with the Phoenicians.

55 Cf., N. Snaith, *The Distinctive Ideas of the Old Testament* (New York: Shocken, 1964), pp. 74-77.

18:25) real judgment and justice cannot be separated from Him Who is the basis of all ethical righteousness.

To the Hebrew mind God's justice (*mišpaṭ*) was not a mere ideal, but an action in time and history. It was manifested in real and observable events because the real God acted with vindicating righteousness upon the deserving (Judg. 5:11).[56] When Israel repented and sought the Lord, He raised up "judges" to accomplish His act of deliverance upon Israel. Thus, the English title "judge," may often be misleading since it conveys the idea of acting mainly in the legal realm in arbitrating disputes between men. Rather, the "judges" were primarily "saviours" or "deliverers" of their people from their enemies.

Actually the noun *šôpēṭ* is not used to describe these men, though the verb "judged" is used of Othniel (3:10), Deborah (4:4), Tola (10:2), Jair (10:3), Jephtah (12:7), Ibzan (12:8), Elon (12:11), Abdon (12:13), and Samson (15:20). Their main duty, then, was the act of "judging" by which they delivered Israel from oppression. As Cundall has shown, the actual "judge" in Israel is the Lord for only He is called *šôpēṭ*.[57] God administered His justice through deliverers whom He empowered with His Spirit (Judg. 3:10).

Davis points out, however, that the judges were called by divine appointment and brought to prominence in the role of a "deliverer" and then later settled as civil leaders.[58] Those who manifested the gifts of the Spirit were called of God and sought out by the people when national emergencies arose. In fact, Deborah was already established as an arbiter of the law in civil matters before she delivered Israel from the Canaanite

---

[56] Cf., comments of G. Vos, *Biblical Theology* (Grand Rapids: Eerdmans, 1949), pp. 270-75.

[57] *Op. cit.*, p. 15.

[58] *Op. cit.*, p. 93. Note that the Old Testament records the years each judge's "judgeship," indicating that he continued to exercise authority after his initial deliverance of the people from oppression.

oppression (Judg. 4:4-5). It is possible, therefore, that Samson did settle down to the quiet life of an arbitering "judge" prior to his escapade at Gaza.

c) The woman of Timnah (Judg. 14:1-15:20)

The events of Samson's life fall into two categories: those prior to the incident at Gaza and those afterwards. However, the narrative divides in relation to the three women in Samson's life. From the start it becomes obvious that a lust for women is his weakness.

The first woman in Samson's life was the Philistine girl from Timnah (or Timnath), a Philistine town only four miles down the valley from Zorah. Despite Philistine domination of the Israelites at that time, Samson was free to stroll through the valley and at Timnah he met the first of his lovers. The proximity of the Danites to the foreigners probably weakened the attitude of separation among the younger generation Israelites, for Samson had no hesitation about marrying the girl though he was breaking the instruction of the Law regarding mixed marriages (Exod. 34:16; Deut. 7:3).

It was unusual for Hebrew children to disobey their parents' wishes, yet, Samson dismissed their displeasure with his choice, saying: "get her for me, for she pleases me well" (Judg. 14:3). His poor and impatient choice is reflected by the fact that the "marriage" was to be a somewhat less than desirable situation. She is described by the common word "woman" and is not designated as a "virgin" or "maiden." Possibly she was a widow or divorcee.[59] Also, the marriage was evidently a "beena" marriage in which the woman remained in her father's house, while her husband visited her with gifts and presents.[60]

---

59 Cundall, *op. cit.*, p. 162, shows that Delilah is called by the same term in 16:4.

60 Cf., comments by R. de Vaux, *Ancient Israel* (New York: Scribner's Sons, 1962), p. 43 and MacKenzie, *op. cit.*, p. 153.

His parents rightly opposed the marriage, but the editor's comment in verse four indicates that God was able to use this human mistake to gain an "occasion" against the Philistines. Looking back over the events, the writer, possibly Samuel, could make this observation.

Samson then traveled down the valley with his parents to Timnah to contract the marriage. Evidently he became separated from his parents and at that time a young lion "roared against him." Moved "mightily" by the Spirit of the Lord he rent the lion in half.[61] The text notes that he had no weapon in his hand, possibly due to Philistine disarmament. It should be observed that the Spirit of the Lord gave Samson unusual strength at the time of crisis.

Sometime after talking with the girl at Timnah, Samson returned alone to the dead carcass of the lion to find that a swarm of bees had made honey in the dehydrated body. By eating the honey Samson deliberately broke one aspect of his Nazirite vow in that he was not to touch a corpse. For this reason he did not tell his parents the source of this gift he made to them.

It was not long until the second part of the vow was also broken for verse 10 states that Samson made a "feast" at the wedding according to Philistine custom, and probably under some pressure from the girl's family and friends. The Hebrew word *mišteh* indicates this was a "drinking feast."[62] There is abundant evidence that the Philistines were given to drinking and carousing. Several beer mugs used for barley beer were found at Tell Abu Hureira (Gerar?),[63] jugs and chalices were turned up at Tell el-Far'ah and Tell en-Naṣbeh.[64] Albright

---

61 This feat is also attributed to David (I Sam. 17:34-35) as well as mythological heroes like Enkidu, Heracles and Polydamas.

62 Cf., comments of Davis, *op. cit.,* p. 136.

63 Cf., Y. Aharoni, "The Land of Gerar," *IEJ,* vi (1956), pp. 26-32, and T. C. Mitchell, "Gerar," *NBD,* p. 463.

64 Cf., C. McCown, *Tell en Naṣbeh,* Vol. I (New Haven: Yale University Press, 1947), p. 95.

suggests that the extensive production of mugs and wine craters gives ample evidence of the Philistine's excessive drinking.[65]

It is also strange that this wedding feast was at the bride's house, rather than the home of the groom. Perhaps Samson's marriage feast was not held in his home because his parents would not sanction the marriage. The length of the feast was seven days, at the end of which the marriage was actually consummated. In this case thirty companions ("sons of the bride-chamber") were selected as a body guard (v. 11) against any who might attempt to plunder the wedding party.[66] Evidently the girl's parents chose the body guard because Samson had not brought any friends with him.

During the opening festivities Samson proposed a riddle to the thirty Philistines to exalt his wisdom. Such procedure was common to the Near East and also to ancient Greece. Because of the Philistines' Aegean origin Samson may have wanted to vindicate himself before them on their own level. The statement of the riddle related to the lion in which he had found the honey: "Out of the eater came forth meat, and out of the strong came forth sweetness" (v. 14).

Unable to discern the meaning of Samson's riddle the Philistines turned to threatening the girl to find out the secret for them. Their threat was to burn her family's house with them in it. So she weeps before Samson to persuade him to tell her the answer. Here the text is a bit ambiguous. Verse 15 states they came to his wife on the seventh day to threaten her but verses 16-17 indicate that she wept and begged him for the answer for seven days. Some have suggested that out of curiosity she begged to know the answer and did not really

---

65 W. F. Albright, *Archaeology of Palestine* (Baltimore: Penguin, 1960) p. 115.

66 Some, however, have suggested that they were chosen as protection against Samson. Cf., the LXX reading "when they feared him."

become urgent until the last day.[67] However, Cassel seems to be more correct when he suggests that verse 15 be translated: "and they had said," indicating that they came to the girl at the first day of the feast when the riddle was put forth and she was not able to discover the answer until the last day.[68] The Philistine men had told her to "persuade" (*p̱aṯiy*, "fool" or "trick") her husband and only her constant recourse to tears moved him to reveal the answer to the riddle. Her claim that he must hate her (v. 16) implies that she used a racial argument to cause him to give in to her demand.

Almost immediately, the Philistines announced to Samson: "What is sweeter than honey, and what is stronger than a lion?" In bitter reply he said: "If you had not ploughed with my heifer, you would not have found out my riddle." Thereby, he clearly indicated that he was aware of the source of their information. The blunder should have forewarned him of one similar, but far worse, that was yet to come. The debt he now owed was substantial. The "sheets" were fine linen pieces worn next to the body and the "change of garments" refers to festival garments, such as those worn to the wedding. Enraged by the events that had transpired he left the wedding to secure payment for the thirty garments, which he obviously did not possess himself. He went to Ashkelon, twenty miles away on the coast, and one of the main cities of the Philistine pentapolis. It lay in a rich, fertile and densely populated area. The Philistines took the city from Judah in the twelfth century B.C. and from there subjugated the tribe of Dan and pushed into the Judean hills.[69] This could give good reason why Samson, a Danite, would choose Ashkelon

---

[67] Cf., comments of Keil and Delitzsch, *op. cit.,* p. 412. It is unlikely, though, that a woman would be that interested in the interpretation of a riddle, for such matters were usually the sport of men.

[68] *Op. cit.,* p. 200.

[69] This view is expressed by M. Pearlman and Y. Yannai, *Historical Sites in Israel* (London: Alden, 1964), pp. 164-70

as the site of his wrath. Cundall also suggests that its distance from Timnah and Samson's yet unknown fame would have made it unlikely that the Ashkelonites would be able to trace him back to the events at the remote outpost of Timnah.[70]

The author notes that the "Spirit of the Lord came upon him" to enable Samson to accomplish the feat of slaying thirty Philistines and using their garments in payment of the answered riddle. Thus, Yahweh found an "occasion" against the Philistines who had dealt treacherously with Samson. However, in the meantime the Philistine girl's father was disgraced by Samson's rude departure and gave the girl instead to the "companion" ("best man") of Samson! Samson must have returned to deliver the garments and in anger went on back to Zorah unaware of what had transpired. Since this marriage was apparently a *beena* marriage, Samson did not intend to live with the girl permanently, but rather, to visit her upon occasion.

At the time of the wheat harvest (Judg. 15:1) Samson returned to visit his wife at Timnah. The time was probably during late May or early June and his anger was now satisfied.[71] He brought the gift of a "kid" (young goat) as the probable "offering" prescribed by the *beena* marriage, in which the wife remained in her parents' home. Thus, Samson visited her in the same way one would visit a prostitute (cf., Gen. 38:15-17).

Upon his return he discovered that his bride had been given to his "best man." In response the girl's father offered Samson her younger sister in an admission that he had acted too hastily. MacKenzie criticizes this account as containing absurd ethics of retaliation.[72] However, Cassel points out

---

70 *Op. cit.,* p. 167. This comment has merit, for it would have been foolish for Samson to attack the neighboring Philistines.

71 Cf., the calculation of this by Cundall, *op. cit.,* p. 168.

72 *Op. cit.,* p. 154. He views the entire account as an "ingenious exaggeration of folklore."

that Samson acted nobly in not harming his fearful father-in-law.[73] Actually it was the Philistines who had initially aggravated the entire situation by threatening his wife. Samson retaliated against the whole group of Philistines in the region by burning the wheat crop. In doing this he turned his personal wrong into an occasion for a national exploit against the enemy of his people.

Until this time Samson had been too free in his association with the Philistines. The disastrous events of his attempted marriage to one of their women turned his attitude against them in such a way that Yahweh could now use him to "begin to deliver" Israel from the Philistines. At this point of the narrative there is a definite break in Samson's relations with the Philistines for the next several years.

Samson was ready to make war but had no soldiers at his disposal. Instead, he turned to the beasts of the field as his confederates. He captured three-hundred jackels (*šûʿāl*) and tied them tail-to-tail in pairs and lit their tails as torches, sending them wildly scattering through the almost-ready-to-harvest grain of the Philistines.[74] Such an act constituted national aggression and made Samson the chief enemy of the Philistines.

The burning of the enemies' crops was always a common method of war in the ancient Near East. It meant total loss to the enemy and in an agrarian culture this was a serious matter. The reference to "shocks" (v. 5) indicated that the grain was already being harvested and stacked in sheaves. The fire spread from the shocks to the standing grain and then to the olive trees.

---

[73] *Op. cit.*, p. 204. Cassel probably has too high a view of Samson as the "noble warrior of God." Yet, it is not necessary to bring him down to the depths of a vagabond rogue. The New Testament lists him as one of the heroes of faith from the Old Testament (Heb. 11:32).

[74] The Hebrew word *šûʿāl* may be rendered either "jackal" or "fox." Foxes are solitary animals found in small families and would be more difficult to catch, whereas, jackals run in packs and are "friendly."

Samson's identity was no secret to the Philistines but they blamed the unwise action of his father-in-law for Samson's retaliation upon them. It is interesting that they did not try to harm Samson who was evidently still in the area (cf., v. 7). Instead, they burned the girl and her father "with fire." Probably they burned their house with them in it; the very fate which she had tried to avert by exposing Samson's riddle! Whatever one may think of Samson's so-called cruelty to the jackals, no one may deny the greater cruelty of the Philistines.[75] The moral implications of the story are very important. First, Samson was wrong in desiring to marry a woman of the enemies of his people and all sorts of terrible repercussions came from his uncontrolled lust. Despite his error, Samson came to see the enemy in the proper light so that God could use him to begin Israel's deliverance. Secondly, the girl should have revealed immediately to Samson the Philistines' threats instead of using trickery to persuade him to divulge the answer to the riddle. The very fate she sought to escape thereby ultimately came upon her anyway. She failed to confide in the trust and protection of her own husband. Thirdly, every aspect of the narrative indicates that the father-in-law acted in haste by giving the bride to the "best man."

In response to the Philistines' cruel murder of the girl and her father, Samson turned upon them. His response to them (v. 7) implies that the cowardly Philistines sought to pacify Samson by their act of cruelty. He announces that he will not cease ("rest") until he has taken vengeance upon them.[76] He

[75] Some feel that far too much has been made of Samson's "cruelty" to the animals he burned. People living in agrarian cultures do not have the extremely sentimental regard for animal life that those in far-removed urban and suburban areas have. The death of animals is common experience in the country. It should also be noted that jackals are undesirable scavengers, as are foxes. Whichever Samson burned he was doing the area a "favor" in ridding it of such pests. In rural areas today such animals are readily shot by farmers!

[76] This reading seems correct in preference to the idea that after he killed more he would then cease. Cf., Keil and Delitzsch, *op. cit.*, p. 414.

then turned on those who had burned the girl and her father and smote them "hip and thigh" (a slang term meaning he beat them "piece by piece").[77]

Realizing the danger he was now in, Samson fled to a cave in the "rock of Etam" which was probably in the cliffs above the Wady Ismaʿin near his hometown of Zorah. In anger the Philistines dispatched a force to capture the Hebrew renegade. They brought soldiers to encamp against Judah in whose territory Samson was hiding. The narrative gives thorough evidence of the timid attitude of the Hebrews to the Philistine menace. The men of Judah criticized Samson for his acts. They said (v. 11): "Do you not know what you have done to us; the Philistines are rulers over us?" Thus, the one-man army found no support even from among his own people. Fearing the threat of war, they begged Samson to leave them and the Philistines alone. This indicates some of the very serious attitudes among the Hebrews of Samson's day. It shows the powerful control and influence of the Philistines over Judah and the failure of the Jews to trust their God. The Philistine encroachment was an ever-threatening menace in those days. Therefore, it is simple to see why Israel needed a deliverer at that time. The subtle Philistine approach would have soon permanently dominated Israel and threatened the life of the nation.[78]

The scene is probably to be set like this: the Philistines camped in the valley before the face of the cliff in which the cave was cut. Similar to many Judean caves, it had to be entered by descending from the top of the cliff and swinging into the mouth of the cave.[79] Evidently the Judeans came to

---

[77] All commentators agree that this phrase is proverbial but none agree as to what it actually signifies. Most take it to mean some kind of total and devastating destruction.

[78] Cf., evaluation of W. F. Albright, *The Biblical Period from Abraham to Ezra* (New York: Harper & Row, 1963), pp. 35-48.

[79] The descriptions of the Bar Kokhba rebels in the caves of Wadi Murabba during the second revolt against Rome. Cf., M. Mansoor, *The Dead Sea Scrolls*

the top of the hill and called down to Samson to surrender. When they promised not to attempt to slay him, he permitted them to bring him up, bind him, and take him to the Philistines.

Verse fourteen states that when they came to Lehi the Philistines shouted against him. "Lehi" means "jawbone" and is used proleptically by the author in anticipation of the event about to happen from which the name was derived.[80] The shouts of triumph by the Philistines brought the manifestation of the Spirit of the Lord upon Samson to move him again with unusual physical strength. He snapped the ropes that bound him, seized the jawbone of a freshly slain ass, and engaged the Philistines with it. Because of his unarmed condition any weapon was a welcome find. The jawbone was evidently that of a recently perished ass that had been picked by the vultures for the jawbone was "fresh" and not brittle. Thus it was not easily broken. Again we see the Hebrews using the most unusual of weapons because of the Philistine monopoly on iron weapons and their policy of disarmament.[81] God would assure all observers that He was able to give victory to His people over all opposing advantages.

Using this unusual weapon Samson slew a thousand Philistines and put the rest to panic and flight. The number one thousand may be a round number for a great host. There are no details given of the battle. The reference to: "a heap, two heaps," may imply that he slew the thousand in several encounters as he pursued the fleeing army. Samson re-

---

Leiden: Brill, 1964), pp. 172-74. Cf., also the entire issue of the *Israel Exploration Journal,* xi (1961), pp. 3-72, which includes the excavation reports of the Bar Kokhba caves.

[80] Keil and Delitzsch, *op. cit.,* p. 416 seem to have been the first to suggest this. Cundall, *op. cit.,* p. 171 follows the same view. Modern critical scholars, though, try to view it as an etiological expression. However, it makes better sense that the place name "jawbone" came after the event rather than the idea that the name already existed and this fantastic story was made up to explain it.

[81] Cf., also Shamgar's ox goad and David's sling used by God to give victory over the heavily armed Philistines.

sponded to his victory in a crude poetic couplet with a play on the words "ass" and "heap" which are identical (ḥ^{a}môr). The idea of the poetic expression was that the red ass' jawbone was used to beat the Philistines bloody red.

The pursuit of the Philistines left Samson exhausted with thirst which is easily explained by the time of year being the hot weather of wheat harvest (v. 1). The overwrought warrior had much to fear for he stood alone in his conflict with the enemy. It is possible that the three thousand men of Judah aided Samson but since there is no mention of this in the text it is unlikely. The entire passage gives adequate evidence of the apathetic attitude of the men of Judah. They were not ashamed to drag their bound hero into the enemy's hands. They were not moved when the Philistines shouted against Samson, and even worse, they apparently made no intervention to aid Samson in the conflict. Their faith in God was so weak that they feared to trust Him even under these circumstances. As great as the triumph of Samson is, the failure of Israel is even greater. Samson was fully conscious that he was fighting for the Lord when he referred to himself as the Lord's "servant" (v. 18) and yet the so-called people of God gave him no aid.

It should be noted that the above incident reveals that Samson's strength was an abnormal human strength and not the magical power of a "superman." After the conflict he was completely exhausted. Through this experience God was trying to teach him the need of relying upon the Lord alone and not upon his own strength and ability. This lesson he apparently did not learn very well.

d) The prostitute of Gaza (Judg. 16:1-3)

The events of Samson's life revolve around the three women of his life of which the Philistine harlot at Gaza was the second. Chronologically, the events of his life divide between the end of chapter fifteen and the beginning of chapter sixteen. The fifteenth chapter concludes with the note that Samson judged Israel "in the days of the Philistines" for twenty years. The Philistine oppression lasted forty years but during the major part of Samson's "judgeship" it appears that he was able to maintain relative peace between Israel and the Philistines for there is undoubtedly a great time lapse between chapters fifteen and sixteen. We may suppose that following the humiliating defeats inflicted by Samson's single-handed efforts, the Philistines no longer undertook to confront him and their penetration of the Judean hill country was temporarily halted. Israel probably enjoyed relative peace and security during these years as a result of the partial "deliverance" accomplished by Samson who remained among his people during these years as a "judge." He either remained in the vicinity of Zorah or possibly lived in Hebron.[82]

Samson's early passion for the woman of Timnah was overcome by his zeal for the Lord. Equipped by God with every necessary potential to be a great leader among Israel, he continued to squander his greatest opportunities to serve the Lord. He who could strangle a lion and kill a thousand men single-handedly could not conquer his own passion and lust. Samson's fall began with a trip to the Philistine city of Gaza. The city of Gaza was the southernmost of the Philistine pentapolis. This ancient city was probably originally inhabited by the Avvim who were later driven out by the Caphtorim (proto-Philistines).[83] It then passed from Amorite to Hyksos to Canaanite control. Joshua conquered Gaza from the Canaanites but later lost it to the Philistines. Tell el-'Ajjul has been identified as most likely ancient Gaza. Excavations

---

82 This is the suggestion of Cassel, *op. cit.,* pp. 211-13. He feels that Hebron served Israel during these years as a makeshift "capital" and that Samson judged the people there. The Biblical text, however, offers no details in this regard.

83 Cf., Deut. 2:23 and the section on Gaza in ch. 3.

there in the 1930's by Sir Flinders Petrie revealed substantial amounts of Philistine pottery.[84]

How it is that the Israelite hero is able to wander casually into this major Philistine city is uncertain. Two things are certain though, that he is an unwelcome guest (v. 2) and that his intentions are not the best. Probably due to an overt sense of pride in his own strength and ability he ventured into the territory of Philistia and came to Gaza. It is unlikely that he went there for the purpose of visiting the prostitute, for he did not see her until after he had arrived (v. 1). One of the great lessons of the spiritual life has always been that one must take heed when he thinks he is standing sure, lest he fall (I Cor. 10:12). Thus, Samson's pride brought him to Gaza and in the weakness of that pride he saw there a *zonāh* and lusted for her in his heart.

As an alien visitor Samson would not have been welcome to remain overnight in the city except at a place such as the house of a prostitute which was always open to strangers.[85] They were a sort of female innkeeper, yet, prostitution was still very much their regular business. Cassel goes to great lengths to vindicate Samson's coming to the Gazite prostitute under these circumstances but his explanation is more ingenious than satisfactory.[86] Every detail of the narrative indicates that his intentions were of the worst sort.

Having seen the *zonāh,* Samson "went in unto her" (*wiyābô'' ēleyāh*). This Hebrew euphemism almost always means that he entered her chamber for the purpose of coming unto her in a sexual relationship. Also, notice that he "lay

---

84 Cf., F. Petrie, *Ancient Gaza,* Vol. I (London: British School of Archaeology in Egypt, 1931) pp. 30 f., and K. Kenyon, *Archaeology in the Holy Land* (New York: Praeger, 1965), p. 307.

85 Such houses were generally built on the back of the walls of the city, not far from the city gates. In Joshua 2, the Hebrew spies were able to find quarters in the house of a prostitute at Jericho. They, however, were not drawn there by sexual impulses.

86 *Op. cit.,* pp. 212-13.

til midnight." If he intended to merely lodge for the evening in this house, why did he arise at midnight to leave? It seems more likely that he went to her house for the single purpose of engaging the woman sexually and then leaving when he was finished.

Even at this low point of Samson's life, God was ready to deliver him from the Philistines. When the men of Gaza found out that Samson was in their city, they came to the gate of the city to wait out the night and ambush him in the morning. Many have questioned how Samson could have carried off the gate while they were there. In verse 2 we find that the Gazites laid in wait for him all night and slept by the gate supposing to take him in the morning when he left the city.[87] Arriving at midnight instead, Samson took them by surprise and carried away the entire gate in which they were

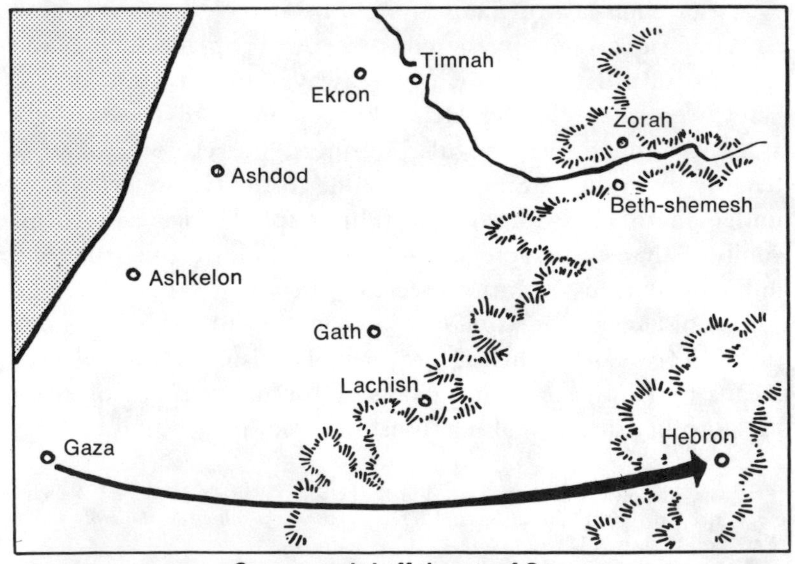

Samson carried off the gate of Gaza

---

87 Thus, the phrase "they were quiet (*hitᵉḥārēš*) all night" indicates that they lapsed into careless repose and most probably fell asleep.

trusting so greatly. In ancient times the gates of walled cities were locked at night and the Gazites probably imagined that Samson could not get out until the gate was opened in the morning, at which time they would be ready for him.

Taking the doors of the gate, the two posts, bar and all; he broke it loose from the wall and carried it away to the top of a hill that was "before Hebron." Hebron was the chief center of the tribe of Judah in those days and may have been Samson's residence during his judgeship. Now Hebron was nearly thirty-eight miles from Gaza and a straight uphill climb from the coastal plain to 3,300 feet above sea level on the crest of the mountains of Judah: an extraordinary feat for any man! The details of the text are not real clear for it is possible that it may mean that Samson carried the gate to the foothills which are before Hebron,[88] or that he carried it to the top of a hill near Gaza "towards" Hebron.[89] However, the statement of the text seems to best be interpreted that he actually carried the gate to Hebron. Consider these factors: (1) once having taken the gate of Gaza as his trophy it would have been more likely that he would want to keep it in mockery of the Philistines; (2) for the gate of Gaza to lie before the Israelite city of Hebron would have marked a sign of triumph over the powerful Philistines; (3) a man who could attack an entire army and without a weapon frighten bands of armed men (Judg. 16:2, 12) could surely carry the gate of Gaza, however heavy it might have been, up to the summit of Hebron.

Despite this triumph, Samson's weakness for Philistine women had again risen and would lead to his humiliation. The beauty and voluptuousness of these women of Greek descent proved more than he could handle. The Hebrew hero

---

88 Cf., J. Davis, *op. cit.*, p. 138.

89 Cf., Cundall, *op. cit.*, p. 175. He defends two views of this matter but does not indicate which he prefers.

that sent fear into the hearts of the Philistine warriors could be conquered by a woman.

e) Delilah of the Valley of Sorek (Judg. 16:4-22)

Delilah is a woman of some mystery in the Old Testament for no one may be certain who she was. The simple statement (v. 4) of the text says she was a "woman of the Valley of Sorek." Most commentators have assumed she was a Philistine, though she is not definitely specified as such. Mac Kenzie has recently suggested that she was actually an Israelite girl.[90] Living in the Valley of Sorek, where both peoples freely mingled, indicates she could have been either Philistine or Hebrew. However, Samson definitely had a passion for Philistine women and it seems unlikely that the five "lords" of the Philistines would venture into Hebrew territory to bribe the girl. Though her name is Semitic in form, the Philistines often borrowed names from the Semitic peoples about them. Whoever this girl was, she was the instrument of Samson's great downfall.

God will not permit his own children to continue indulging in sin without soon receiving the stinging results of such experimentation. Twice before Samson's passion had led him into the place of danger and this was to be the last. The escape at Gaza had taught the mighty warrior nothing about God's patience to deliver his erring soul. That Delilah was a professional prostitute is obvious from the context.[91] Her residence in the Valley of Sorek placed her near the hometown of Samson at Zorah.

Almost immediately the "lords of the Philistines" came to bribe Delilah into discovering the secret of Samson's strength. It is most likely that these were the five lords of the pentapo-

---

[90] *Op. cit.,* pp. 155-56. He suggests that since she is not specified as a "Philistine," as the other two women of Samson's life, she was not one.

[91] Cf., MacKenzie, *ibid.*

lis (*sarnê pelištîm*) who visited her. They each offered to give her 1,100 pieces of silver, which would have been an offer of 5,500 pieces of silver for betraying Samson into their hands.[92] They evidently recognized Samson to be no giant or "superman" and because of this they rightly assumed his abnormal strength to come from another source. They wrongly, however, thought it to be from some external magical charm or amulet. Such superstitious gimmicks were worn frequently by the Philistines themselves when they went into battle (II Sam. 5:21). They carried their idols with them on their battle campaigns intending these portable images (*aṣabîm*) to serve as good-luck amulets.[93] However, Samson's strength was the result of the moving of the Spirit of the Lord upon him and this was connected to the provisions of his Nazirite vow.

Delilah immediately set out with ruthless efficiency to procure the "secret" from Samson. Moved by the desire to satisfy his own lustful passion Samson became blinded to the real motivating force behind her continuous questions. It should be noted that her repeated attempts to find the answer indicate that he was in the habit of visiting her regularly so that she could continually pursue the matter. One should not overlook the brutal cleverness of Delilah. With the heartlessness of a professional prostitute she used her "trade" to lull Samson into sleeping passivity. The full context shows that she could "read" him clearly. She knew the three times he lied to her before she ever attempted to prove them false and she knew the time he was finally telling her the truth (v. 18).

Delilah's playful pleading to know the source of his strength brought equally jesting remarks from Samson. The

---

92 This is an incredible amount compared with the thirty pieces of silver for which Jesus was betrayed by Judas Iscariot.

93 R. A. S. Macalister, *The Philistines: Their History and Civilization* (London: British Academy, 1913), p. 91. He notes that they continued the practice for several centuries (cf., II Macc. 12:40).

first suggestion he gave her was to bind him with seven "fresh bowstrings" (RSV). Now the reader should carefully notice the details of the text. After this disclosure the lords of the Philistines brought her the bowstrings to try on Samson. They also left men to lie in wait to ambush Samson once the secret was discovered. Upon her next opportunity Delilah bound the sleeping Samson and called: "the Philistines are upon you" and awaking from his sleep he immediately snapped the bow strings (v. 9). The text does not say that the liers-in-wait actually came upon him but only that she screamed: "the Philistines are upon you." Had these men rushed into the room three times after Samson's disclosure of the "secret" he would surely have been suspicious of Delilah's treachery. This writer believes they never actually engaged him the first three times.[94]

The second playful suggestion by Samson was to bind him with new ropes (v. 11) which had failed to hold him years earlier (15:13). Again Delilah tied him up and cried out in pretense of attack to expose his lie. Attempt number three brought Samson perilously close to the truth when he told her to pin his hair into the mechanism of a weaver's loom. He was now more near the truth about his hair. The loom in her house was probably vertical and the two posts were fixed in the ground and fastened by a crossbeam from which the warp threads were suspended. Apparently she wove Samson's long hair into the warp and pinned it in the web so that it resembled a piece of cloth. Upon her screaming again, Samson awoke and jerked his head pulling the hair out of the loom, pin and all! Cundall asks the interesting question: "one wonders who was kind enough to disentangle Delilah's labours?!"[95]

---

94 This writer knows of no other recent commentator taking this position. Though it is alluded to by H. Steenstra, the translator of Cassel's commentary on Judges in the Lange series: *op. cit.*, p. 215.

95 *Op. cit.*, p. 177.

From this point Delilah, who had willingly played games with Samson's half-hearted replies, began to put the pressure on him. "You have mocked me these three times . . . how can you say 'I love you,' when your heart is not with me?" (v. 15). One can easily imagine her tears freely flowing to reinforce her plea to the ever more tenderhearted Samson! Her nagging became so incessant that "she pressed him daily with her words and urged him, so that his soul was vexed unto death" (v. 16). She literally "nagged him to death!" What man could stand up under such an attack?!!

This became the turning point of the entire situation. He then revealed all his heart to her concerning the Nazirite vow and presumably the fact that the uncut hair was the only remaining sign of his consecration to Yahweh. Verse eighteen is the key to understanding the entire account: "and when Delilah saw that he told her all his heart, she sent and called for the lords of the Philistines, saying: Come up this once for he has showed all his heart." The prostitute could read his emotions clearly and she now knew he was no longer jesting with her and had surely emptied his heart to her in foolish trust. Therefore, she called the lords themselves to come up this one time to take him and also to bring the money with them for she was convinced that Samson had revealed the truth to her. Poor unsuspecting Samson! His disregard for his consecration to the Lord would now lead to the removal of the last sign of the Nazirite vow and render him useless to the Lord's service.

It is a poor understanding of the theology of this account to declare Samson to have thought his strength lay alone in his uncut hair. Every mention of his physical prowess is accompanied by the remark that the Spirit of the Lord came upon him to move him to such great physical strength. The importance of the uncut hair was that it was one of the signs of the vow; in fact, it was the only one of the three signs that was outwardly observable. He himself stated to Delilah that a haircut would break the vow and render him powerless because physical strength was the particular gift he had from God as a result of consecration to Him. His loss of strength afterwards was also clearly attributed to the departure of the Spirit from him (v. 20).

It is most likely that Delilah used sexual intercourse to induce heavy sleep upon the mighty Samson and he slept through the haircut. Delilah, greedy for the great reward of silver, sat calmly, conscious of the awful fate to which she was delivering her "lover." The utter heartless cruelty of Delilah, so typical of a prostitute, is revealed in the phrase: "and she began to afflict him" (v. 20). Delilah herself beat Samson back to consciousness and she called in mocking tones: "The Philistines are upon you, Samson." In reality the only Philistine attacking him was Delilah herself! When he awoke, Samson doubtless leaped up supposing this to be another gag whereby she had somehow bound him and said: "I will go out as at the other times and shake myself free" (v. 20).[96]

The brief note at the end of v. 20, has to be one of the saddest comments in all Scripture: "and he knew not that the Lord had departed from him." The special manifestation of the Spirit of Yahweh as the fulfillment of the Nazirite vow was now gone, for the last provision of Samson's consecration had been broken. The self-sufficient warrior thought he could still exert his strength and did not immediately perceive that it was gone.

---

96 H. Steenstra adds this note to Cassel's comments on v. 20: "He (Cassel) supposes Samson to see the Philistines, and to express his determination to give them battle as heretofore. But not to say that *ninéar* will not bear this sense, it seems clear that the "other times" refer to the previous attempts of Delilah to master his secret. Cf., Cassel, *op. cit.*, p. 215. Thus, *ʾinā̄ṣē̄r* means that Samson thinking himself to be bound again in some manner determines to shake himself loose.

f) Samson's humiliation and revenge at Gaza (Judg. 16:21-31)

God had patiently dealt with Samson after he touched the dead lion and drank wine at the feast, but now as the outward sign of Samson's Nazirite vow disappeared, His patience turned to judgment and Samson was utterly powerless without the help of the Lord. The lords of the Philistines rushed in for the first time and took Samson in Delilah's chamber and put out his eyes and then bound him with "fetters of brass" (*n*^{e}*ḥuš*^{e}*ṯaîm*). The dual form may suggest he was bound hand and foot or that he was bound doubly secure.

The Philistines brought Samson to Gaza in this state of utter humiliation. The very city whose gate he had recently carried away now welcomed its blind captive. Samson's future potential was now annulled. His uncontrolled lust had placed him in a condition where God could no longer use him to battle the Philistines hand to hand, for he was blind. He had disqualified himself by his selfish sin.

The Philistines allowed him to live and chained him to the grinding mill where he ground out the grain by hand.[97] This was the most tedious and lowest kind of slave labor and was usually the work of women slaves (cf. 9:53). Thus the Philistines brought Samson to the depth of utter humiliation. In the now hollowed sockets of his eyes he carried the mark of his shame and unfaithfulness as God's servant. Although his hair is said to have begun to grow again, he was not likely in prison very long before the Philistines brought him forth to celebrate their victory. There is also no evidence that the growing of his hair caused him to receive any strength until after he called upon the Lord (v. 28).

---

[96] It is very unlikely that he ground at an ox or ass mill for his strength was no longer abnormal and such large, animal-powered mills did not exist until the fifth century B.C. MacKenzie, *op. cit.,* attempts to connect this with the ass mill, but there is no basis for this claim from the evidence of archaeological finds.

The Philistines credited their new acquisition to their god Dagon as a victory over Yahweh of the Hebrews. So the lords of the pentapolis gathered at Gaza for a great feast to praise Dagon. Dagon was the Semitic grain deity whom the Philistines had borrowed from the Canaanites. Earlier commentators thought Dagon to be a fish deity (from the Hebrew *dāg*),[98] but modern Semitic studies have shown "Dagon" to be derived from the word *dāgān* ("grain").[99] He was probably, therefore, part of the fertility pantheon of the Canaanites. In Ugaritic literature he appears as the father of Baal. "Dagon" appears in name forms as early as the third millennium B.C. (Idin-Dagan and Isme-Dagan).[100] It is interesting to note the Philistines believed that by grinding out the grain Samson was acknowledging the supremacy of Dagon over him!

The Philistines' great mistake was thinking that their god had delivered Samson into their hands (v. 23). Yahweh could not permit this allusion. He had delivered his faithless servant into their hands but would yet find one more "occasion" against the Philistines because of Samson. At the peak of the revelry of the feast to Dagon, they called for Samson to "make sport" or entertain them. Every Philistine could dare mock and curse the helpless blind hero who was made to put on a performance for the crowd.

The "house" was probably the pillared temple of Dagon where the lords and rulers were in the covered section below, while the crowd of guests was upon the roof (v. 17) watching

---

[98] Cf., Keil and Delitzsch, *op. cit.*, p. 424 and Cassel, *op. cit.*, p. 222, for ingenious but erroneous explanations of this concept.

[99] Cf., Albright, *Archaeology and the Religion of Israel* (Baltimore: John Hopkins Press, 1953 ed.), pp. 74 and 220, n. 15. Also *BDB*, p. 186, and K. A. Kitchen, "Dagon," *NBD*, pp. 287-88. Cf., also M. Delcor, *Jahweh et Dagon; ou le Jahwisme face à la religion des Philistins de'après* I Sam. V," *Vetus Testamentum,* xiv (1964), pp. 136-54.

[100] For details on early evidence for the name *Dāgān* see Macalister, *op. cit.*, p. 108.

Samson in the courtyard below. Cundall notes that the great host of people upon the roof may have made the whole structure unstable.[101] After the "performance" Samson was chained to the pillars just under the edge of the roof, being led by a young boy. The details of the temple's structure are unknown as is the matter of exactly how pulling out two pillars could collapse the whole structure. Such pillars, though, were common to Philistine temples built around courtyards.[102]

The humiliating consequences of Samson's sin must certainly have caused him to do some serious thinking and probably moved him to repentance. The very fact that he prays to the Lord (v. 28) gives some evidence of spirituality. This is the only recorded prayer of Samson that we have in Scripture. Despite the six-fold use of the personal pronoun the prayer is a sincere request of God to allow Samson to do the only thing he now could do in his state of blindness. He calls upon God using three different titles: Adonai, Yahweh, Elohim.

Samson asked the lad who guided him to place him at the central pillars. After his prayer he took hold of the two middle pillars, bowed himself forward, sliding the pillars off their stone bases, and brought death to a great host of the Philistines, especially those under the roof (v. 30). How many were killed is not specified except that the number was more than he had previously killed during his lifetime.

Dr. Cassel must be given credit here for an ingenious observation. He asks the question: "Who furnished the report of the last hours of the hero's life?"[103] If this is no mere folk

---

[101] *Op. cit.*, p. 180. This observation does not deny the validity of the miraculous feat which follows, but rather notes how such a feat was accomplished, for no mere human effort could pull down such a structure.

[102] *BA*, xiv (1951), p. 44.

[103] *Op. cit.*, p. 224. The heartwarming conjecture that follows is most plausible indeed.

legend, how were the details reported? Cassel observed that the lad (*na'ar*) who led the blind Samson by the hand was probably a Hebrew slave, for surely they would have feared to let a Philistine boy near the Hebrew rogue. The boy may even have been Samson's attendant who willingly stayed with him in the prison. Knowing what he was about to do, it is unlikely that Samson would have let the boy die with him. Yet the lad could have reported the events of the feast and Samson's prayer when he escaped to home.

After Samson died with the Philistines in the collapse of the temple of Dagon at Gaza, his fellow-countrymen came to bury his dead body. This is the first hint of any action on their part. Perhaps this was their first glimpse of the need to stand up for Yahweh against the enemy. Times of catastrophe and death are times of mitigated hatred on the part of both bereaved groups. The Philistines evidently made no attempt to refuse Samson a proper burial in his family tomb.[104] Samson's father Manoah was probably deceased by this time for he is not said to have come himself. The reference to Samson's "brethren" must be to his tribal countrymen since he was an only child. They buried Samson in the hill country overlooking the Valley of Sorek, the very scene of his greatest triumphs and his greatest failures!

The Biblical writers do not hesitate to record valid history that includes both the triumphs and failures of its "heroes." No attempt is made to conceal the moral impurities of Samson. Thus Garstang concluded that there is no reason to doubt the original authenticity of Joshua-Judges.[105] Samson's spiritual failures are not condoned by the text, rather, they are the means of his downfall. He is a tragic picture of

---

104 They were not so kind to Saul in later times (I Sam. 31:9-10).

105 J. Garstang, *Joshua-Judges* (London: Constable & Co., 1931), p. 341. For an excellent discussion of the proper approach to the study of Old Testament history cf., R. de Vaux, "Method in the Study of Early Hebrew History," in P. Hyatt (ed.), *The Bible in Modern Scholarship* (New York: Abingdon, 1968), pp. 15-29. He criticizes the negative approaches of Von Rad, Mendenhall, and Noth.

the man of God, fully equipped to serve the Lord but whose service is rendered ineffective by his passion and lust.

I SAMUEL

The Philistines take the major role in the First Book of Samuel as the chief enemies of Israel. In these chapters we see the crucial conflict that brings Israel to the point of national crisis. Out of this national calamity arose Israel's great deliverer, King David. The book opens on a disastrous note as the Philistines capture the Ark of the Covenant.

The capture of the Ark of the Covenant (I Sam. 4:6)

The history of Israel recorded by Samuel is not comprehensive, but rather, selective as he writes from a theocratic-prophetic point of view with an emphasis upon the Kingdom of God. The sovereignty of God clearly permeates the narrative. Because of the great sin into which Israel had lapsed, God permitted her to lose temporarily her most valued possession, the Ark of the Covenant. The ark was the visible representation of God's presence among His people and was in the tabernacle at Shiloh.[106]

Samuel had advised Israel to engage the Philistines in war several years after the time of Samson. Israel was now awake to the threat of Philistine domination and ready to try to halt it. However, the corruption of the priesthood by Eli's two sons and the complacency of the old priests would bring this effort to failure. The defeat of Israel's army and the consequent loss of the ark of Yahweh brought God's judgment upon the house of Eli. What Samuel and Israel were to learn

---

106 The finest study available dealing with the theological significance of the ark is M. Woudstra, *The Ark of the Covenant from Conquest to Kingship* (Philadelphia: Presbyterian & Reformed, 1965). He discusses all the views of the construction and appearance of the ark as well.

from this crisis was that deliverance from the enemy's oppression depended upon spiritual conversion.

Israel took the initiative in the battle to halt Philistine encroachment in her territory. The Israelite army encamped at Eben-ezer and the Philistine army at Aphek. When the battle ensued four thousand men of Israel fell. In an attempt to remedy this initial setback the elders of Israel decided to take the Ark of the Covenant before them in battle. Nothing can be more clear than the fact that they did wrong by removing the ark from the tabernacle at Shiloh. Yet, in the ultimate outcome the sovereign God caused this action to be the very thing that spared the ark.

The Philistines, as has already been mentioned, placed great emphasis upon the use of images and magical amulets which they carried with them into battle to secure the favor of the gods. It is likely that the Israelites' desire to take the ark with them was strongly influenced by the Philistine practice. When the ark was brought into the Hebrew camp the people gave such a great shout that it caused the ground to tremble. However, this only caused the Philistines to be all the more determined to defeat what they called the "gods" of Israel.

When the battle came thirty thousand men of Israel were slain, Eli's two sons were killed, and the ark was captured by the Philistines as the men of Israel fled in retreat. When word of the loss of the ark came to the aged Eli at Shiloh he fell over backward and broke his neck and died. His forty year judgeship ended and most commentators presume that the Philistines pushed on to Shiloh and destroyed the worship center and the tabernacle with fire.[107]

---

[107] The Danish excavation under Hans Kjaer excavated Shiloh (Tell Seilun) from 1926-29 and again in 1932, revealing that it certainly had been destroyed by fire in c. 1050 B.C. which was undoubtedly the work of the Philistines. Cf., Kjaer, "The Excavation of Shiloh, 1929," *The Journal of the Palestine Oriental Society*, x (1930), pp. 87-114. On the Tabernacle see F. Cross, "The Tabernacle," *BA*, x (1947), pp. 45-68.

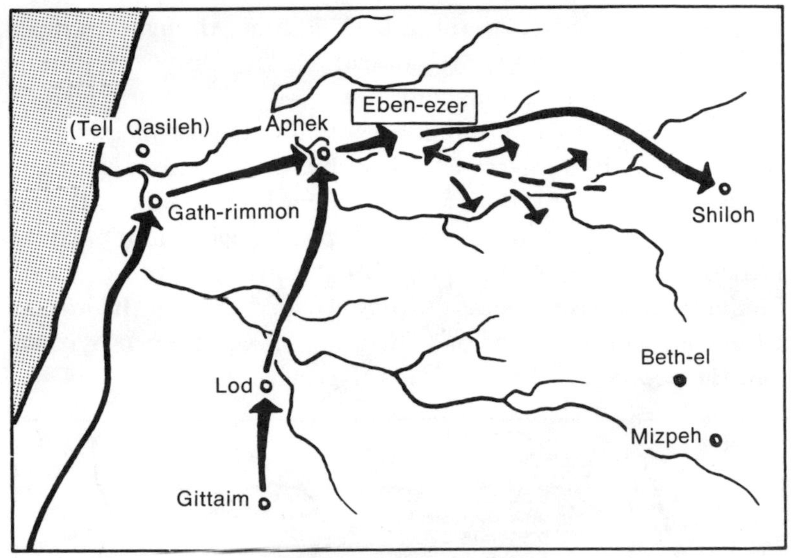

Battle of Eben-ezer and the destruction of Shiloh

Jeremiah 7:12 makes clear the fact that God permitted the destruction of Shiloh in judgment of Israel. While the ark was in the hands of the Philistines there was no mention of Samuel's activity in Israel. For seven months the ark remained in Philistine territory (I Sam. 6:1), being taken first to the temple of Dagon at Ashdod on the coast.

The temple of Dagon at Ashdod had become the chief center of Dagon worship after Samson's destruction of the temple at Gaza. The Philistines placed the ark of Yahweh beside the image of Dagon, possibly to signify it as an offering to Dagon. However, the next morning they found Dagon fallen face down before the ark of the Lord. The words: "and they took Dagon, and set him in his place again," must have struck a note of humor to every Israelite who read this account. The helpless Dagon could not stand before the living God of Israel. The following morning proved even worse for the Philistine priests as they found Dagon again on his face before the ark. This time, though, his head and hands were "cut off' (*k^erutôt*).[108] Only the stump (*ḏāgôn*) of the image remained intact.

Along with this humiliation of the Philistine god, the people of Ashdod were stricken by fatal tumors. In their desire to get rid of the troublesome ark they sent it to the border town of Gath where the people were immediately inflicted with severe hemorrhoids ("boils in their secret or hinderparts"). In desperation they decided to send the ark on to nearby Ekron but its bad fortune was well known by then and the people of Ekron refused to receive it.

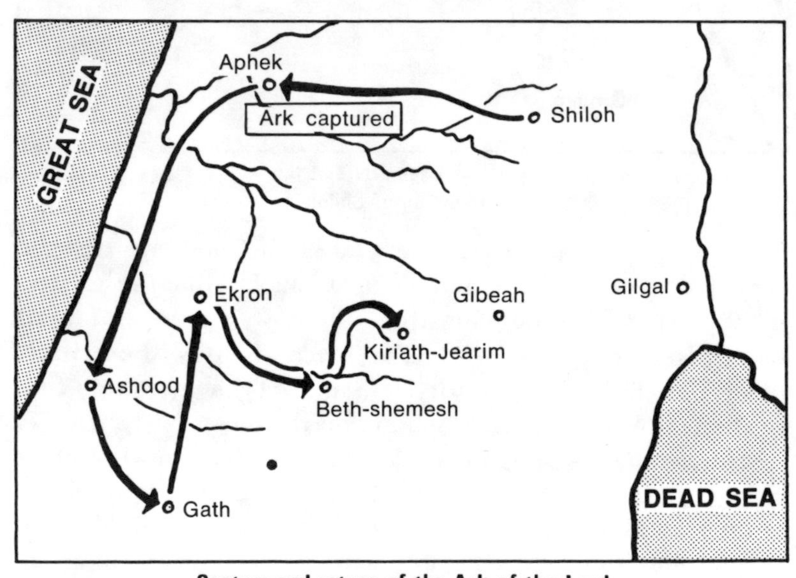

Capture and return of the Ark of the Lord

Thereupon the Philistines decided to return the ark to the Israelites for it had brought them nothing but trouble for seven months (I Sam. 6:1). Their priests, however, warned

108 Any naturalistic explanation of how the idol may have fallen and broken is unnecessary since his hands and head were not broken but "cut-off."

them to send a trespass (*ā̌sām*) offering with it in the hope of compensating Yahweh. They decided to send five golden boils (A.V.-"emerods") and five golden mice along with the ark. These representations of their plagues were thought by pagan peoples to bring healing from the thing represented. The mice may indicate that they suffered from the bubonic plague. The number five images were corresponding to the five lords of the Philistines.

The Philistines planned to return the ark on a new ox cart[109] which would be drawn by two young "milch" cows that had never been yoked. The "milk cows" were to put Yahweh to the test. Naturally they would return to their young sucklings and not wander off into Israelite territory. It was a clever attempt to test the power of the God of the Israelites to cause the cows to pull the ark back to Israel. The practice was part of the Philistines' pagan Aegean heritage, yet Yahweh used it to His own advantage. Parallels to this procedure may be found in ancient Greek legends where Dionysos tells Cadmos that he and his wife were turned to serpents and driven in a wagon led by two young cows, and where the wagon stopped they built a city.[110] Then the cows were sacrificed to Athena, just as people of Beth-shemesh sacrificed them to Yahweh. The city built by Cadmos in the Homeric legend was Theba which is derived from the Greek word for "ark" (*tēbā*).[111] The word may

---

109 Such ox carts are represented in the mural inscriptions of Ramses III at Medinet Habu. Cf., Garstang, *op. cit.*, p. 338. For a picture cf., ch. 3.

110 Euripides, *Bacchae*, 1333-35. A similar thing happened to Cadmos in Phoenissae, 640. For a thorough discussion of these matters see M. Astour, *Hellenosemitica* (Leiden: Brill, 1967), pp. 157-58. He, however, attempts to make the practice originate in Israel and transfer to the Greeks on the basis that *ā̌sām* implies the whole narrative is Hebraic. However, if the practice were Hebrew, and not Philistine, why is there no other evidence of such a practice among the Hebrews? The text clearly indicates that the entire procedure was the Philistines' idea.

111 The word *tēbā* ("ark"), however is probably derived from the ark of the "local Noah," King Ogygos, who survived a great flood.

also mean "chest." Notice that the Philistines put jewels in a small "chest" and put it on the cart with the Ark of the Covenant (v. 8).

The whole procedure was to prove whether Yahweh had inflicted them and wanted the ark back in Israel or whether all these calamities had happened by chance (v. 9). The cows went straight to Beth-shemesh in the area of the Valley of Sorek. The lords of the Philistines followed the ark to that point and fled home after observing the rejoicing of the Israelites.

The people of the city were down in the valley reaping the wheat harvest when they saw the ark coming. This was probably during the month of May. When the cart stopped before a large rock, they chopped up the wood and offered the cows in a burnt-offering to the Lord. The writer notes that the stone in the field of Joshua of Beth-shemesh remained until his own day (v. 18). Unfortunately the Israelites did not treat the ark with as much respect as the Philistines had, for the men of Beth-shemesh looked inside it and 50,070 died; and they too sent the ark away, calling upon the people of Kirjath-jearim to come for it. This city was the closest to the location of the ruined Shiloh and inherited the ark of the Lord for the next twenty years. At Kirjath-jearim it lay in neglect as ample testimony to the failure of the amphictyony.[112] The "judges" were not able to establish Israel in the land for the people had rejected the Lord. Soon the cry for a king would arise from the citizens.

2. Samuel's victory at Mizpeh (I Sam. 7:1-17)

Twenty years had passed since the failure of Israel at Eben-ezer and now Israel was finally ready to meet the Philistines at Mizpeh under the prophet-judge Samuel. He had

112 Cf., the helpful comments of J. Bright, *A History of Israel* (Philadelphia: Westminster, 1959), pp. 164-66. He observes (n. 7) that Saul did not have the actual ark with him in 14:18, but an "ephod."

been functioning as a circuit judge administering the covenant law among the tribes.[113] Samuel called the people to spiritual renewal in preparation to meet the Philistine threat. He called upon Israel to put away the strange gods they were worshiping: Baalim and Ashtaroth (v. 3). These were not only the gods of the Canaanites but also of the Philistines themselves.[114] Israel was so dominated by the Philistine aristocracy that they had not only submitted to their political influcnce but also to their religious influence. Certainly we see here the lowpoint of these people in their spiritual relationship to Yahweh. Baal was the Semitic fertility god adopted by the Philistines and was prominently worshiped at Ekron.[115] Ashtoreth was the chief Semitic fertility goddess and was also borrowed by the Philistines.[116] Israel could not hope for victory while she continued to worship her enemies' gods!

The people responded and cast away their idols and "served the Lord only" (v. 4). Samuel commanded all Israel to gather at Mizpeh where he would pray for them. Mizpeh (or Mizpah) was a small town on the Benjamite-Philistine border and has been identified in modern times as Tell En Nasbeh from the excavations of Yale University and the American Schools of Oriental Research.[117] At Mizpeh they poured out water unto the Lord in an act of surrender to God and confessed their sin before the Lord, and "Samuel judged the children of Israel in Mizpeh" (v. 6).

---

[113] Cf., M. Noth, *"Amt und Berufung im Alten Testament,"* in *Bonner Akademische Reden,* xix (1958), p. 21.

[114] Cf., ch. 2.

[115] Macalister, *op. cit.,* p. 92.

[116] She appears with several similar names throughout Semitic cultures as Asherah, Ashtart, Anat, Ahirat, etc. The best discussion available of this deity is J. B. Pritchard, *Palestinian Figurines in Relation to Certain Goddesses Known through Literature* (Philadelphia: University of Pennsylvania, 1943).

[117] Cf., report by C. McCown, *Tell En Nasbeh,* 2 vols. (New Haven: Asor, 1947). Ample evidence was found to indicate a settlement there in Samuel's time. They found Philistine pottery there resembling Mycenaean LH III C, p. 94.

When the Philistines heard of this gathering they sent against Israel the five lords of the pentapolis with their armies. Samuel quieted the frightened Israelites and promised them victory. He offered a burnt offering to the Lord as the Philistines approached in the distance and the Lord "thundered with a great thunder on that day upon the Philistines" and threw them into confusion (*y^e^humēs,* cf., Josh. 10:10). The men of Israel rushed out from Mizpeh upon the panicked Philistines and chased them back into their own territory, recovering the Israelite cities up to the borders of Gath and Ekron. Excavations at Tell Qasile, the Philistine port north of Joppa on the Jarkon River, show that it was destroyed in the middle of the eleventh century (stratum XI) probably by the Israelites at the time of Samuel's victory.[118]

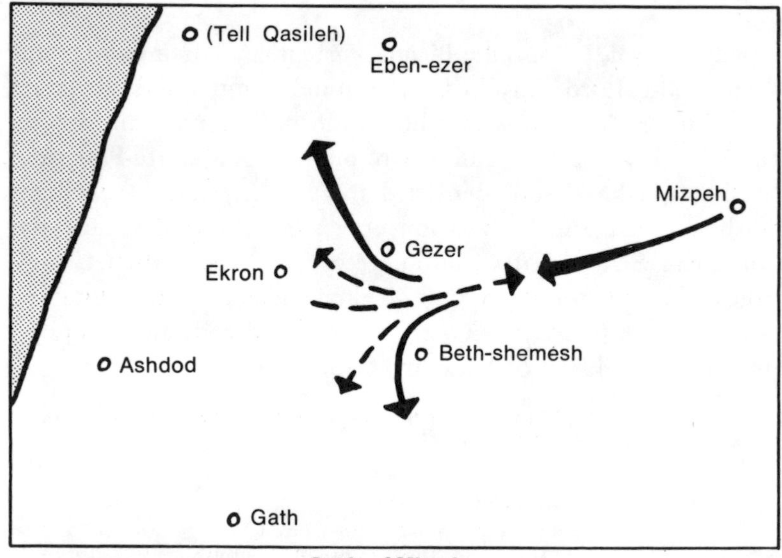

Battle of Mizpeh

---

[118] Cf., G. E. Wright, "The Archaeology of Palestine," in *The Bible and the Ancient Near East* (Garden City: Doubleday, 1961), pp. 116-17, and Y. Aharoni and M. Avi Yonah, *The Macmillan Bible Atlas,* p. 58.

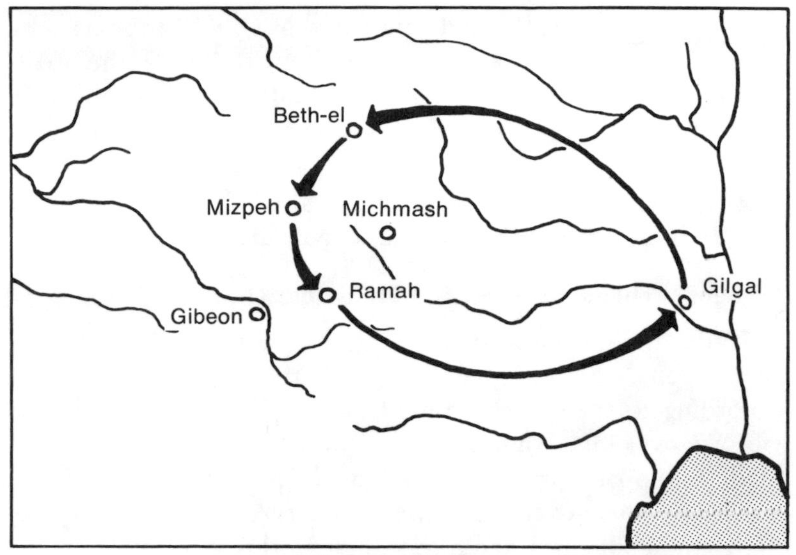

Samuel's Circuit

Samuel set up a stone between Mizpeh and Shen and called it Eben-ezer ("stone of help") saying: "hitherto hath the Lord helped us." This name is the same as that of the place of Israel's defeat twenty years earlier. It had taken that long for the nation to learn the need of spiritual preparation for military victory. From this time onward the Philistines were no longer able to bring all Israel under their domination (v. 13), though they made intensified excursions into the hill country. These were met by Israelite defiance and the apathy of Samson's day was now long passed.

As a result of Israel's victory even the powerful Amorites left them alone and a time of "cold war" followed during which Samuel traveled a circuit from his home town of Ramah to Gilgal, Bethel, and Mizpeh. Upon his return to Ramah he would judge Israel there. As a "judge" Samuel also functioned as a prophet and a priest and held authority over all Israel. It is likely that the "school of the prophets" in later years (II Kings 2:1, ff.) had originated at Gilgal in the days of Samuel. MacKenzie feels this "institution" was the main factor which prevented Israel from falling under Philistine control.[119] These "sons of the prophets" emerged to proclaim that Yahweh was the God of Israel. Standing for the traditions of the Law they were also a major factor in repudiating Canaanite religion and civilization.

3. Saul's rebellion against the Philistines (I Sam. 13, 14)

Under the constant pressure of the people for a king "like the nations," Samuel installed Saul, the Benjamite, as king according to the commandment of God (I Sam. 8). His initial victory over the Ammonites at Jabesh-Gilead (I Sam. 11) made him prominent in the eyes of the people. The desire for a king by the people was the direct result of the conflicts with the Philistines and the constant threat they posed to Israel. Recent evidence has shown that there was actually a Philistine-Ammonite alliance at that time and the two nations were pressing against Israel from both directions.[120]

The Philistines comprise the majority of the narratives dealing with Saul. He came to reign with great potential. He valued sacrifice before engaging in battle (I Sam. 13); he opposed sin (I Sam. 14); he banished wizards out of the land (I Sam. 28); and in general observed the Mosaic law. However, his good intentions turned to miserable failure in the pursuit of the Philistines (I Sam. 14) and the war with the Amalekites (I Sam. 15). His hasty acts of self-will and self-

---

[119] *Op. cit.,* pp. 174-75. His comments are very helpful here, though, he foolishly denies the historical existence of Samuel. Cf., also A. Weiser, "*Samuels Philister-Seig; die Uberlieferungen in* I Samuel VII," *Zeitschfiftfür Theologie und Kirche,* lvi (1959), pp. 253-72.

[120] This is suggested by G. E. Wright, "Fresh Evidence for the Philistine Story," *Biblical Archaeologist,* xxix (1966), pp. 110-34. He shows how the Philistines were also pushing southward in the upper Jordan Valley in an attempt to divide Israel for conquest. On the Ammonites, see G. Landes, "The Material Civilization of the Ammonites," *Biblical Archaeologist,* xxiv (1961), pp. 2-9.

gratification ultimately brought his own death and the failure to inflict any permanent defeat upon the Philistines. Thus, Samuel's initial hesitation to grant the people a king was vindicated by subsequent developments. Mendelsohn has effectively shown why he would denounce a kingship based on the excesses of the Canaanite concept which they knew.[121] It is very strange indeed that the desire of the Israelites to have a king to lead them in battle arose from the conflicts with the Philistines who had no king themselves![122] The desire for a king was not so wrong as the improper motivation that lay behind the desire: failure to trust the Lord as their God-King.

The establishment of a kingdom meant open rebellion against the Philistine over-lords. Saul took two thousand men up to Michmash while his son Jonathan rallied one thousand at Gibeah (Saul's capital in Benjamin). Jonathan struck first and routed the Philistine garrison at Geba and killed the governor there. Meanwhile Saul had assembled the people at Gilgal to prepare to go up to Michmash but he had to wait for Samuel to come to offer sacrifice to the Lord. While they waited, the Philistines assembled at Michmash. I Samuel 13:7 states that the people followed Saul "trembling" with fear. He waited at Gilgal seven days "according to the time that Samuel had appointed (v. 8), but Samuel did not come and the people began to desert Saul. At the end of the day Saul himself intruded into the priest's office and offered the sacrifice. "And it came to pass, that as soon as he made an end of offering the burnt-offering, behold, Samuel came" (v. 10). He denounced Saul's impatience and announced that his

---

121 Cf., I. Mendelsohn, "Samuel's Denunciation of Kingship in Light of the Akkadian documents from Ugarit," *BASOR,* 143 (1956), pp. 17-21. He shows that Samuel's warnings about kingship were true to the type of practices being used by contemporary Canaanite rulers.

122 Cf., the helpful comments of B. Rahtjen, "Philistine and Hebrew Amphictyonies," *Journal of Near Eastern Studies,* xxiv (1965), pp. 100-104.

line would not continue in the kingship and the Lord would seek another to be king.[123]

The Philistines sent out three raiding parties ("spoilers") from Michmash into Israelite territory. At this point the author notes that the Philistines had previously disarmed the Israelites (vv. 19-22). They had kept tight control of the iron monopoly so that the Hebrews had only two weapons (v. 22) and were dependent upon the Philistines to sharpen even their farm implements. As a result of this policy of disarmament only Saul and Jonathan had swords and armor. This is probably why Saul himself offered his armor to David at a later time (I Sam. 17). It was all the Israelites had!

The Philistine raiding parties were sent out to force Israel

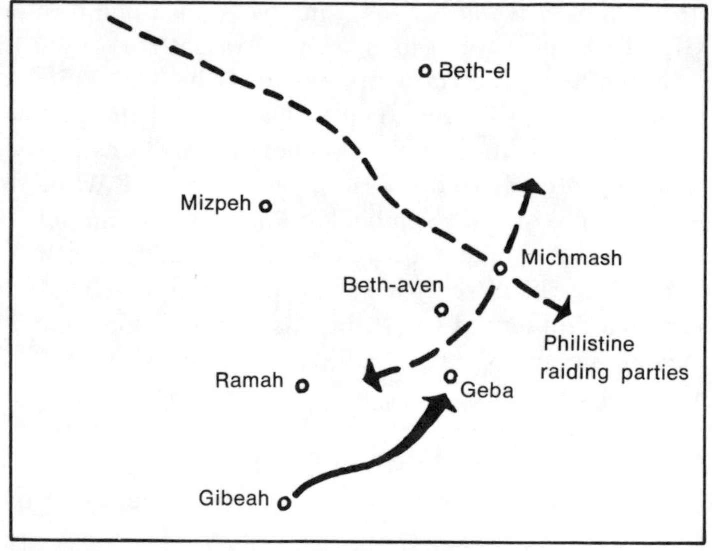

Jonathan's victory at Geba

---

123 This is the view of C. Keil and F. Delitzsch, *Biblical Commentary on the Books of Samuel* (Grand Rapids: Eerdmans, 1950 reprint of 1857 ed.) pp. 129-30. He lost the perpetuity of the kingdom on this occasion and later lost it for himself as well.

out of the strongholds of Gibeah and Geba into battle. They set up a guard at the pass of Michmash to protect the main camp. Saul had come from Gilgal to Gibeah and finally joined Jonathan at Geba, opposite Michmash. The deep Wadi Suweinit with its steep sides separated the two armies.

Overconfidence led to a poor move on the part of the Philistines. Instead of concentrating their main force at Michmash, they remained divided and spread out over the land. In an act of great courage Jonathan took his armor-bearer and sneaked across to the Philistine outpost and "told not his father" (I Sam. 14:1). The passage consisted of sharp rock on both sides and the two Israelites climbed up the facing with the words: " . . . it may be that the Lord will work for us; for there is no restraint to the Lord to save by many or by few" (v. 6). They allowed the Philistines to spot them and were challenged them to come up to them. Jonathan said to his companion: "Come up after me: for the Lord has delivered them into the hand of Israel" (v. 12). Climbing up hand and foot they reached the top and fought back to back (v. 13) and slew about twenty men of the guard. At this point there was an earthquake which threw the Philistines into confusion and Saul led the army out of the camp and chased them beyond Beth-aven and thus "the Lord saved Israel that day" (v. 23).

Saul's forces pursued the Philistines into the region of Aijalon. The Philistine army consisted partly of Hebrew mercenaries who then joined Saul (v. 21) in the pursuit. In Saul's desire to annihilate the Philistines he pronounced a curse of death upon anyone who stopped the pursuit to eat. However, at the end of the day the famished army slew the spoil of animals on the open ground and ate them raw with the blood.[124] Saul's order had actually caused the people to sin against the law of the Lord (v. 33 ff.).

---

124 Astour, *op. cit.*, pp. 178-79, tries to claim that this event was a religious sacrifice parallel to the tearing in pieces and eating of the raw flesh of the victim

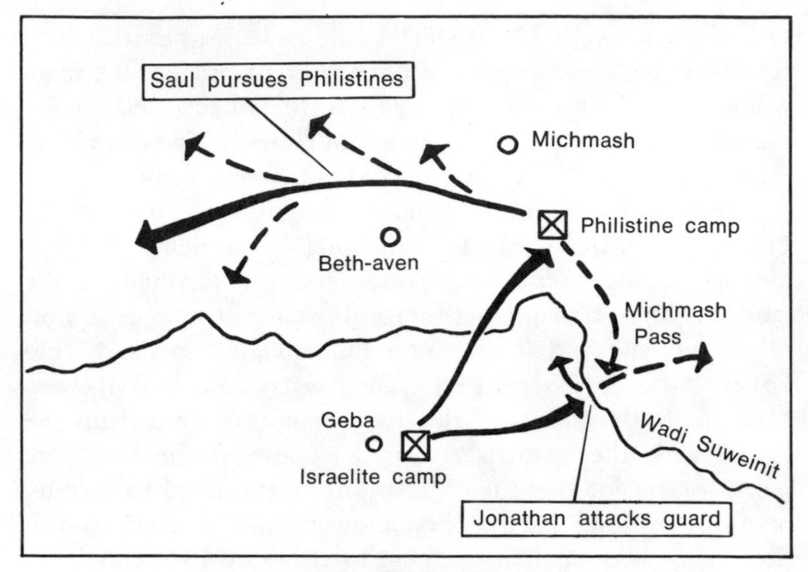

Battle of Michmash

Saul had established his kingdom in Israel but constant war with the Philistines continued throughout his reign as he was never able to bring them to total defeat. He defeated many other nations, including the Amalekites (I Sam. 15), but again he sinned against the Lord (v. 19). That Saul was an unsaved man seems obvious from the events of his life. He is an excuse-maker (I Sam. 15:21); an evil man (I Sam. 16:14); a very jealous person (I Sam. 18:8, 9); and a murderer (I Sam. 19:1). The Amalekite war became the turning point of his career. Samuel recognized that the Lord was against Saul and departed from him for rejecting the word of the Lord (I Sam. 15:26). As Samuel walked away, Saul reached out to

---

in essential rites of the Greek, Bacchic orgies related to the Dionysiac-Orphic cycle and also attested in Crete. He also interprets Samuel's carving up of Agag, the Amalakite King, as preparation for sacrificing him to Yahweh! However, this denies the context of hunger and exhaustion in which Saul's men ate the raw animals and the sin that was attached to this act. As to Samuel, human sacrifices to the Lord were forbidden in Israel.

grab his robe ("mantle") and it tore. Samuel replied that the Kingdom of Israel was rent from Saul that day and given to another (v. 28). Samuel went home to Ramah and never came to see Saul again (v. 35). Evidently the next time Saul saw the old prophet was when he came up from the dead at En-dor wearing the torn mantle (I Sam. 28:14) and reminded Saul that the kingdom had been rent from his hand (v. 17)!

4. David and the Philistines

Samuel was led by the Lord to anoint David, the son of Jesse of the town of Bethlehem, as king. However, it would be ten years before David would come to the throne of Israel at about age thirty. When Saul was terrified by an evil spirit David was brought to play before him for he was a "cunning player." Saul was soothed temporarily and made David his armor-bearer. Ancient kings had many armor-bearers, though, and David returned home forgotten by Saul.

a) David's victory over Goliath (I Sam. 17)

Sometime later Saul confronted the Philistines near the outskirts of Gath where they were preparing to attack the mountains of Judah. The Philistine camp was at Ephes-dammim between Shochoh and Azekah overlooking the Valley of Elah. The army of Israel encamped on the other side of the strategic valley. The valley was especially important for military purposes because it gave access to Hebron, Bethlehem, and the Judean hills. It was probably named for numerous terebinth (*elah*) trees which once grew there. The author reiterates the importance of the valley being between them (v. 3), for this is where David was to meet Goliath alone.

In the Philistine army there was a Gittite named Goliath who stood about nine foot, three inches tall ("six cubits and a span"), and who was recognized as their "champion."[125] He is described in verses 5-7, as a typical Aegean warrior. He wore a bronze helmet that was probably feathered in Philistine style. The Homeric heroes also wore bronze helmets that flashed in the sun and were topped with a crest of horsehair.[126] He wore a "coat of mail" and Achaeans usually appear in Homer's tales as "bronzeshirted."[127] It was the product of great technical skill and had to be light-weight as well as durable. He also had "greaves of brass" upon his legs as the Achaeans in Homer, who frequently calls them: "well-greaved." Such equipment appears often in Mycenaean art of the LH III C period, and Philistine pottery seems to have borrowed these decorations.[128]

Goliath's spear was the unique feature of his equipment. It was large and heavy (the head weighted 600 shekels) and complicated.[129] The iron head was new to the Israelites. The shaft compared to a weaver's beam (leash rod) and it has been suggested that this is a reference to "loop javelin" popularly used by the Greeks. Using the woven loop, the warrior would insert his fingers into it and, thereby, throw the spear a great distance.[130] Thus equipped, Goliath was no

---

[125] He was probably a descendent of the Anakim who were a race of gigantic people.

[126] For an excellent survey of Goliath's armor see E. Yamauchi, *Greece and Babylon: Early Contacts Between the Aegean and the Near East* (Grand Rapids: Baker, 1967), pp. 45-56. Cf., also F. Stubbings, "Arms and Armour," in A. Wace and F. Stubbings (ed's.), *A Companion to Homer* (London: Macmillan, 1962), p. 515. He notes finds of such helmets at Ilaysos, Dendra and Knossos.

[127] *Ibid.*, p. 505.

[128] *Ibid.*, Cf., examples found at Enkomi in Cyrpus and Khalandritsa in Achaea.

[129] Yamauchi, *op. cit.*, notes that the champions of the Iliad also carried gigantic spears (Ajax and Achilles).

[130] Cf., C. Kraft and J. MacKenzie, *Judges-Samuel in the Illustrated Encyclopedia of the Living Bible*, Vol. IV (Chicago: San Francisco Productions, 1967), pp. 78-79. It is impossible to determine whose comments these actually are since dozens of Hebrew and American editors contributed to this project.

even match for the poorly armed and thoroughly frightened Israelites.

Goliath challenged the army of Israel to select a champion from their ranks to confront him (v. 8) in a battle of championship (v. 9). The single combatants would decide the fate of each army. The individual victor would bring victory to his army and the loser would cause his people to go into slavery. He defied Israel to send forth her man but all of the Israelites were afraid. If anyone were to answer this challenge, it should have been newly-elected King Saul, the leader

Greek warrior armed in a manner similar to that of Goliath. Reproduced from a Rhodian painting on the inside of a plate (Sixth century B.C.). Notice the loop-javelin in his hand.

of Israel who stood "head and shoulders above any man in Israel" (I Sam 9:2).

The concept of victory by championship battle is definitely Aegean and again substantiates the origin of the Philistines. Achilles and Hector fought in such contests in Homeric legends.[131] Livy tells of the champions of the Loratii and the Curiatii.[132] Parallels may also be found among the Hittites of Asia Minor, the same area later occupied by the Trojans. The Hittites had teams of champions similar to David's twelve men of II Samuel 2:12.[133]

The concept of such a battle was based upon the Philistine concept of religion. They believed in the power of all gods to chose to aid the armies of men. The Canaanites viewed each "god" as being able to aid only "his" country. The Hebrews believed Yahweh was the only God and could give victory to whomever He chose. To the Philistines a battle of champions would test the favor of the gods. If the gods could give the champion victory, they could give the entire army victory. Therefore, the test of the conflict was a test of the power of the gods. This explains why Goliath made a mockery of the God of the Israelites (v. 45). If He could not empower their champion, how could He give victory to their nation?

It has always been questioned why Saul would allow a youth, despite his confession of faith in Yahweh, to represent Israel in such a contest. It should be noted that up to that point the battle had been at a standstill for at least forty days (v. 16). Neither side had been able to gain a victory. Saul was not always a man of his word and it is quite likely that, though he hoped David would win, Saul never intended to

---

131 Cf., *Iliad,* XXII:273 ff. Even Hector's taunts are similar to those of Goliath, reflecting the common culture of both.

132 Cf., quotations in Livy I:23.

133 Cf., the comments of H. Hoffer, "A Hittite Analog to the David and Goliath Contest of Champions" in the *Catholic Biblical Quarterly,* xxx (1968), pp. 220-25. He feels this recent discovery is the closest Near Eastern parallel to the context of I Samuel 17.

give up to the Philistines if David did not defeat Goliath. Notice that the Philistines fled away when they saw Goliath fall. Why? Because they recognized the validity of battle of championship. They believed that Yahweh had defeated their gods, and so they ran. Saul, therefore, had nothing to lose but David. He knew that if the Lord enabled David to win the Philistines would accept the results of the contest and either surrender or flee. If David were to have lost, Saul could still have kept the Philistines at a standstill. The fact that even the Philistines violated the challenge and ran indicates the Hebrews probably would have violated it also, since it was not their idea in the first place. Bringing all this into consideration resolves many of the apparent "problems" in this passage.[134]

Three of David's older brothers were serving in the army under Saul while he, being the youngest, stayed home to care for the sheep. His father sent him to take provisions to his brothers. David arrived just as they were going into battle. With the recklessness of youth, he ran into the midst of the army (v. 22) and there encountered Goliath's challenge for the first time, though Goliath had given it many times before. Saul, meanwhile, was seeking a man to confront Goliath but none was found despite the rewards which included marriage to the king's daughter (v. 25).

Despite criticism from his oldest brother (v. 28), David volunteered to fight Goliath with the words: "Is there not a cause?" He recognized that there was a reason or purpose for someone to stand up for the Lord. It was his strong conviction of faith in God that stopped the mouths of his critics. Saul also was reluctant to let David fight because of his lack of experience (v. 33). David replied that God had helped him slay a lion and a bear which attacked his father's sheep, and

[134] Cf., for example W. F. Albright, *Archaeology and the Religion of Israel*, p. 70. He unnecessarily doubts the historical validity of the narrative. J. Bright, *op. cit.*, pp. 171-72, however, is inclined to accept it.

"this uncircumcised Philistine shall be as one of them, seeing he has defied the armies of the living God" (v. 36). Saul could reply only: "Go, and the Lord be with you."

Having refused the offer of Saul's armor, which was probably one of the few sets possessed by the disarmed Israelites, David took his shepherd's staff and selected five smooth stones from the brook to use with his sling. David went forth into the valley to face Goliath with courage and agility and confidence in the intervention of God on his behalf. He had to separate himself from the cowardly and unfaithful army of Israel and go forth alone to meet the Philistine champion.

The sling that David carried was no mere toy. It had long been used as a weapon by warriors, shepherds, and hunters. It was composed of three parts: (1) the sling strap, made of leather or cloth, (2) two thongs to give momentum to the strap, and (3) the sling stone. The stone was placed in the strap and held firm by the left hand. With his right hand the slinger would stretch the thongs above his head, whirl and sling, release the end of one of the thongs, thereby sending the stone hurtling toward its target.[135] Though it was still used as a weapon (cf., I Chron. 12:2) it was hardly a match for Goliath's size and cumbersome equipment.

Seeing someone descending into the valley, Goliath got together his regalia and set out to meet him, only to discover that he was being confronted by a teen-ager! Goliath mocked the Israelites for sending such a youth to fight him and "cursed David by his gods."[136] Then he threatened to kill David but the young man replied that Yahweh would deliver Goliath into his hands and that he would kill Goliath. Amid this episode runs the theocentric viewpoint that: "the Lord

[135] Y. Yadin, *The Art of Warfare in Biblical Lands* (London: 1962), p. 80 ff.

[136] Goliath's actions parallel those of Hector in *Iliad* (13:831-2). The reference to *maqelot* ("sticks"), seems to be a jibe at David's shepherd staff. Also read the idea that Goliath cursed David by his own God, Yahweh, and was thus defying the God of heaven. Cf., Keil and Delitzsch, *op. cit.*, p. 183.

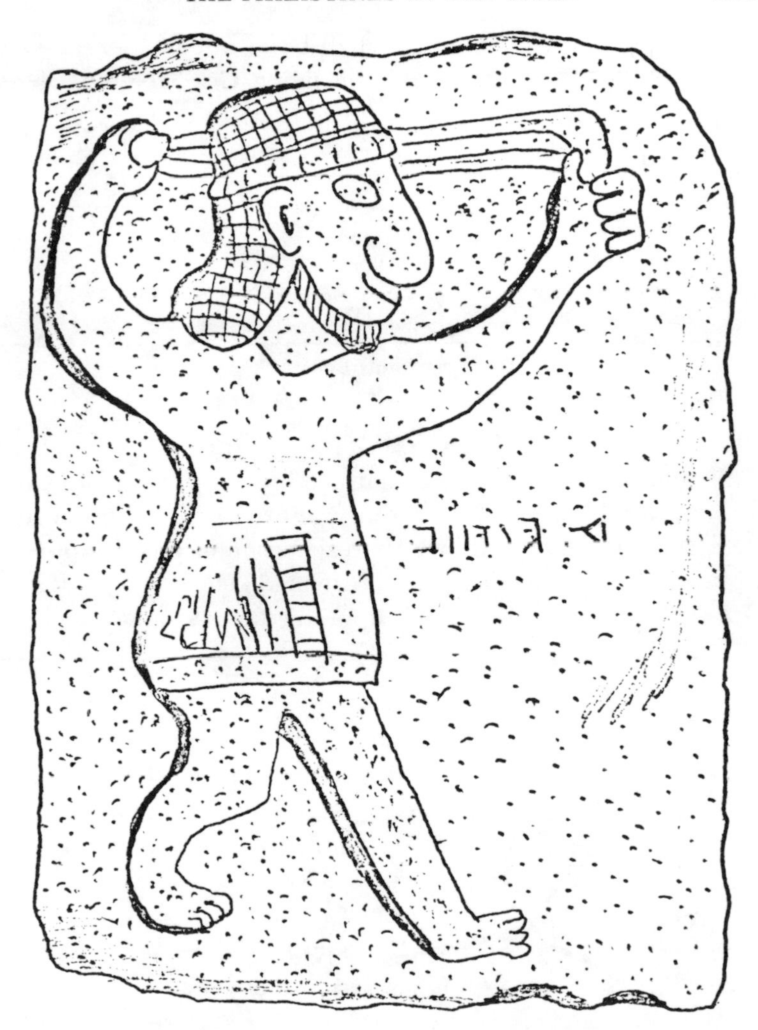

Slingman depicted in Royal Palace at Tell Halaf (10th century B.C.)

saves not with sword and spear; for the battle is the Lord's" (v. 47). Goliath did not turn in disgust, but stayed to fight the outspoken young man. When Goliath approached him, David ran right toward the giant in total abandonment to the

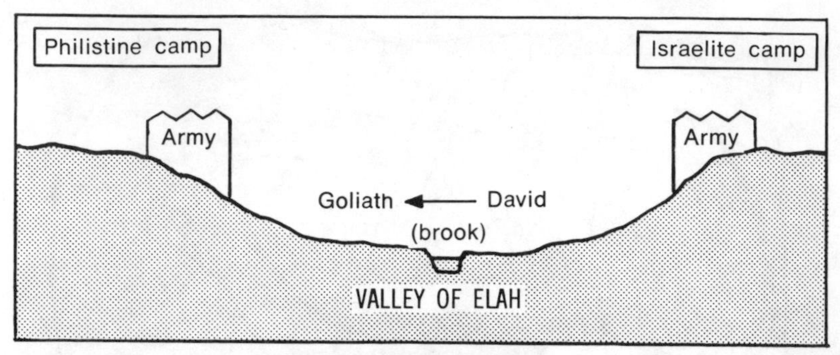

David confronts Goliath

will of God to save him. Verse 48 says that he ran toward the Philistine army to meet Goliath. Thus, he was practically running uphill to confront him. Failure at this point would have cost David everything. He reached in his pouch, found a stone and slung it at the giant's forehead. The stone sunk into Goliath's forehead and he fell upon his face. Strange weapons

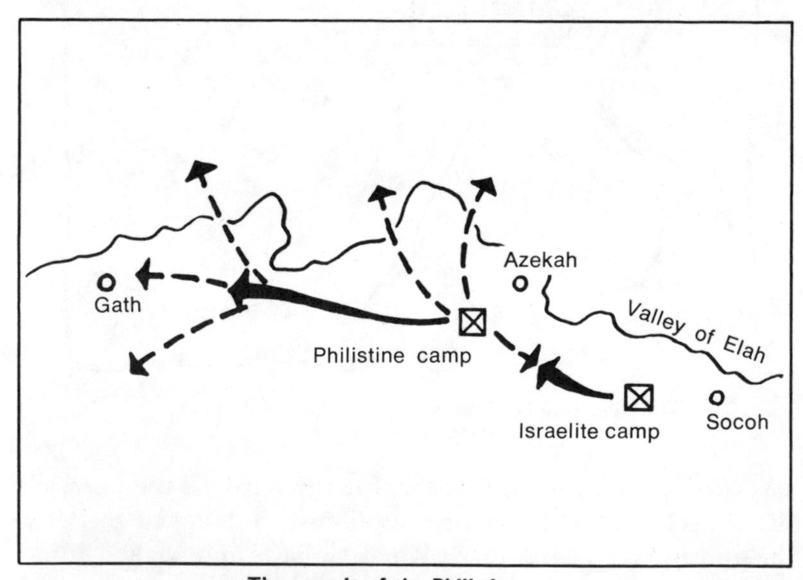

The pursuit of the Philistines

are used by God to equip His servants so that He may receive the glory.

Goliath had been struck in one of the few vulnerable and unprotected spots on his body and lay lifeless (or nearly so) upon the ground. David ran and stood upon the gigantic warrior, took Goliath's own sword and cut off his head with it. When the Philistines were certain that Goliath was dead, they fled and, finally, the men of Israel pursued them back to Gath and Ekron.

David took the head of Goliath to the Canaanite stronghold of Jerusalem as a symbol of Israelite triumph.[137] However, David kept his armor in his own tent, probably because of the lack of metal armor and weapons in Israel. The major problem with this passage is Saul's question (v. 55): "Whose son is this?" Many have supposed a contradiction here with chapter 16 in which David was already known to Saul and now Saul asks who he is.[138] This was not, however, the intention of his question. What Saul asked was who David's father was (*ben-qîzeh,* "who(se) is this son"). Some have proposed that David now had a beard and looked quite different to Saul or that Saul was under fits of madness before and had now forgotten David. These explanations are unlikely since David's brothers brought him to Saul. It is true that David went back and forth from Saul to keeping his father's sheep, but Saul still probably knew who David was. The real question had to do with his father's house.[139] Saul

137 This explanation seems best. Keil and Delitzsch, *op. cit.,* pp. 184-85, try unnecessarily to explain that the city was Israelite while only the citadel was Jebusite. David wanted the Jebusites to see what he had done.

138 E.g., cf., J. Bright, *op. cit.,* p. 171. He clearly states that chapter 16 "cannot be harmonized" with chapter 17. This seems to be a very biased statement since many satisfactory harmonizations exist. It seems that Bright actually rejects harmonization without considering it!

139 Saul has sent to Jesse for David (I Sam. 16:19) but only at the suggestion of his servant. Most likely he did not know Jesse at all by name and the servant himself became the messenger who went to Jesse since he knew him.

had promised to the man who slew Goliath the freedom of his father's house (I Sam. 17:25). That prompted the question about the boy's father, to which David replied: "I am the son of thy servant Jesse the Bethlehemite" (v. 58). He made no mention that his name was David probably because Saul already knew that. Notice the context. Saul immediately decided not to permit David to return home any longer (I Sam. 18:2). Presumably Saul had Jesse informed of his intention to keep David among his soldiers. All these things required Saul to know the name of David's father.

Saul set David over the men of war and gave him his daughter, Michal, in marriage. However, he had become jealous and fearful of David and required a wedding dowry of one hundred Philistine foreskins, hoping that the attempt to kill so many Philistines would cost David his life (I Sam. 18:25). However, David and his men slew two hundred Philistines and Saul was obliged to give Michal to David. When Saul realized that the Lord was with David, he feared him the more.

In the following months Saul attempted to kill David three times by throwing the javelin at him, but each time he missed and David escaped. Perhaps this was a loop javelin captured from the Philistines and Saul was not skilled in using it. Finally David fled to the prophet Samuel at Ramah. When Saul attempted to take David there, Saul was overcome by the Spirit and lay on the ground in a helpless state of ecstasy.[140] Even Jonathan, who loved David greatly, could no longer protect him and David was forced to become a fugitive. He went to Ahimelech, the priest of the sanctuary at Nob and there obtained provisions by eating the "holy bread" (I Sam. 21:6) and also acquired the sword of Goliath

---

140 For a discussion of prophetic ecstasy in Israel and its difference from that of other Near Eastern nations see L. Wood, "Ecstasy and Israel's Early Prophets," *Evangelical Theological Society Bulletin*, ix (1966), pp. 125-38; R. Alden, "Ecstasy and the Prophets," *Ibid.*, pp. 149-56.

that he had placed there in dedication to the Lord. David did not permit religious conventions to overrule the practical needs of the man of God. Again notice that there was no sword at Nob except that of Goliath (I Sam. 21:9). The unarmed David took it for his protection.

b) David the fugitive (I Sam. 21-26)

Taking the sword of Goliath who was from Gath, David foolishly went directly to Gath. When he arrived, though, he feared Achish the King of Gath and feigned insanity outside the gate of the city and Achish let him escape to the cave of Adullam (I Sam. 22:1). This spot was on the border between Philistia and Judah. It has been identified as Tell esh-Sheikh Madkur in the hills overlooking the Valley of Elah. The city was well populated in ancient times and was a natural fortress for refuge. Here nearly four hundred men gathered with David. Among these were his own brothers (I Sam. 22:1) and all sorts of renegades.

David sent his parents into Moab for protection and at the instruction of the prophet Gad moved into the forest of Hareth in Judah. Saul mobilized his forces against David and in the process discovered from Doeg the Edomite that the priest at Nob had aided David (v. 9). Saul ordered that all eighty-five priests and their families be slain at Nob (v. 17-18). However, one priest, Abiathar, escaped to David and remained with him (v. 23). David then realized that he had caused the death of all the priests and promised protection to Abiathar.

War with the Philistines came to play a major part in David's life during the time of his wanderings. He heard that they were robbing the threshing floor at Keilah and took his men there to stop them and save the Israelites (I Sam. 23). Instead of being grateful to David for his help, Saul attempted to capture him there and kill him (v. 8). Again David was forced to flee and escaped to the Wilderness of Ziph.

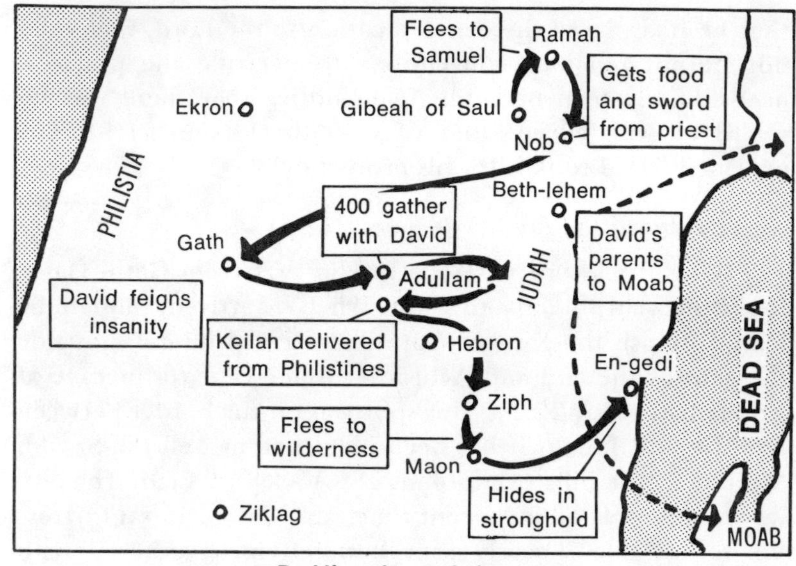

David's early wanderings

Here Jonathan sneaked away and met David and encouraged him (v. 16, 17). The picture of his devotion to David is heartwarming indeed, in contrast to the greed of Saul. With no selfishness at all on his part Jonathan said: "You will be king over Israel, and I shall be next unto you" (v. 17). After renewing their covenant Jonathan returned home while Saul continued to pursue David.

The Ziphites then conspired with Saul to betray David to him (v. 19). Saul hypocritically and almost blasphemously replied: "Blessed are you of the Lord; for you have had compassion on me" (v. 21). David, however, withdrew to the Wilderness of Maon (v. 25) and Saul pursued him there. Just as Saul's men had about surrounded David, word came that the Philistines had invaded the land and Saul had to turn away from David to stop the Philistines. David went further into the wilderness near the Dead Sea to the stronghold of En-gedi.[141]

After the Philistine conflict, Saul again sought David and came into the region of En-gedi. These are the caves of the Dead Sea area, where the barren cliffs overlook the sea. Here there was an oasis to sustain them. The cliffs were called *meṣadoṯ* ("strongholds") because they were natural fortresses. The caves were also natural sheepfolds and are still used as such by the Bedouins today. When Saul came to such a cave, he entered in to rest from the pursuit (v. 3). It turned out to be the very cave in which David and his men were hiding.

David's men encouraged him to kill Saul immediately but he refused to put his own hand against "the Lord's anointed." Instead, he cut off the bottom of Saul's robe while he slept. When Saul arose and left the cave, David ran out and waved the piece of robe and pleaded his innocence, showing he had no desire to harm Saul. The king very typically responded in an emotional manner, but still did not repent; even though he acknowledged that David would one day be king (v. 20).

Soon afterward the prophet Samuel died and David moved into the Wilderness of Paran. The death of Samuel became the breaking point for Saul because no one was left to bring God's message any longer. Again in chapter twenty-six, the Ziphites betrayed David's presence among them to Saul and he went after David with 3,000 men. That night they camped in the trench before the Hill of Hachilah. While they were asleep, David and Abishai crept into the camp and took Saul's spear and cruse of water (v. 12). Again David refused to take Saul's life and said: "The Lord shall smite him (v. 10). Then climbing a distant hill, David cried to Abner, the king's

141 This is the same place where the Bar Kokhba rebels hid during the second Roman Revolt.

bodyguard, about his failure to protect Saul. He asked Saul why he insisted on hunting him and trying to drive him out of his own country. Saul again had his usual emotional response: "I have sinned: return my son David . . ." (v. 21). But David knew better than to trust the unrighteous Saul and responded: "The Lord render to every man his righteousness and his faithfulness." Saul returned to Gibeah but David decided to make a totally different move and fled into Philistia!

c) David among the Philistines (I Sam. 27-31)

Fearing that Saul would eventually catch up with him, David decided to become a Philistine mercenary, knowing that Saul would not dare pursue him there. He went to Achish the King of Gath (probably an underlord to the five lords of the pentapolis) and took six hundred men with him. Achish accepted him this time since he was obviously Saul's enemy. He followed the principle that the "enemies of my enemies are my friends." David was given the town of Ziklag in the Negeb to dwell in with his family (I Sam. 27:6). David's sojourn in Philistia lasted sixteen months (v. 7).

While at Ziklag, David invaded the land of the Amalekites who were mutual enemies of Israel and Philistia. He also, however, destroyed the Geshurites and the Girzites who were probably the allies of the Philistines.[142] He left no survivors and Achish never found out that he was actually fighting for the benefit of Israel. It is clear from the text that there was not a large Israelite settlement in the Negeb in David's time and the archaeological evidence from the area bears the same conclusion.[143] Glueck found no population of any density

---

[142] The best archaeological information available on this period of David's life is the work in the Negeb by N. Glueck, *Rivers in the Desert* (New York: Farrar, Straus & Cudahy, 1959), p. 124 ff. He accepts the validity of David's exploits in the Negeb.

[143] *Ibid.* Cf., also H. Kassis, "Gath and the Structure of the Philistine Society," *Journal of Biblical Literature,* 84 (1965), pp. 259-71.

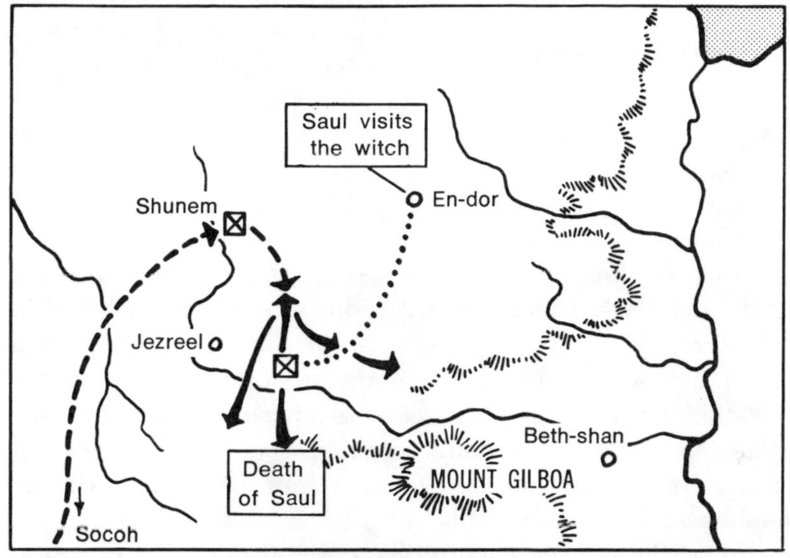

Battle of Mount Gilboa

settled in the area in the Early Iron Age. The Negeb of Judah included the Negeb of Caleb, the Yerahmeelites, and the Kenites. These tribes tented within the territory of Judah and were the allies of Israel. Thus, Achish believed the Israelites must have hated David and he, thereby, had gained a new servant for life (v. 12).

A turning point in David's relations with the Philistines came in the Battle of Mount Gilboa (I Sam. 28). The Philistines mobilized their forces northward and camped at Shunem (v. 4), while Saul's army was on the slope of the mountains of Gilboa near Jezreel. Aharoni suggests the order of events began with the movement of the Philistines to Aphek in the Plain of Sharon and then an advancement along the Via Maris to Shunem at the Hill of Moreh.[144] Meanwhile Saul moved opposite them in the mountainous region of Gilboa to neutralize their heavy equipment.

---

144 *Macmillan Bible Atlas*, p. 64.

Shunem lay near the Valley of Jezreel, the famous battleground. Nearby was the fortified city of Beth-shan over which they had control.[145] From there they could raid the Israelites in the hill country. The intention of the Philistines seems to have been to cut off Judah from Galilee.

The thought of the coming conflict left Saul stunned (v. 5: "his heart greatly trembled"). He realized this would be a serious conflict and he had no message from the Lord ("neither by dreams, nor by Urim, nor by prophets"). In desperation he revealed his ungodly heart by seeking out a witch at nearby En-dor to attempt to recall Samuel from the dead. Even she was surprised and screamed when Samuel really did arise and instantly she knew who Saul was (v. 12). Samuel evidently appeared far different from any hoax she had ordinarily conjured.[146]

Samuel's only message to Saul was a reminder that God had torn the kingdom out of his hand and given it to David (v. 17). He announced to Saul that he and his sons would die the next day in battle (v. 19). Nevertheless, Saul went forth into the battle without seeking God's forgiveness and pardon.

In the meanwhile, Achish had commanded David to fight beside him in the battle and David had almost no choice but to battle his own people until Yahweh providentially overruled the situation. When the Philistines had gathered at Aphek to prepare to move up to Shunem, the lords of the Philistines refused to permit David to go with them (I Sam.

---

145 On Philistine influence at Beth-shan see A. Rowe and G. M. Fitzgerald, *Beth-shan,* 4 vols. (Philadelphia: University of Pennsylvania, 1930-31). Cf., I, p. 38; II, pp. 22-35. There is extensive evidence of Philistine pottery at Beth-shan as well as clay coffins of Philistine mercenaries. Pere Vincent suggests the mercenaries took the citadel at the time of Ramses III and later allied with the surge of incoming "Sea Peoples" cf., *RB* (1923), p. 436. Two temples were found there which may be those of Ashtoreth and Dagon.

146 A fair evaluation of the text must admit that the Hebrew writer was not so superstitious as to believe the witch could raise a prophet from the dead.

29). They criticized Achish for bringing along the six hundred Hebrews and ordered him to send them home.

When David returned to Ziklag he discovered that the Amalekites had raided the town and burned it. They had also carried away the women and children as captives (I Sam. 30:3). David's wives Ahinoam and Abigail were also taken. The Israelites were so upset that they even considered stoning David (v. 6), but he "encouraged himself in the Lord his God." David asked Abiathar the priest to enquire by the ephod to discern God's will and the Lord promised victory and full recovery of all that was lost.

David went south with six hundred men to pursue the Amalekites but by the time they came to the Brook Besor two hundred were too exhausted to go on with them. They came upon an Egyptian then who had been left behind ill by the Amalekites and he guided them to the Amalekite camp. The feasting raiders were taken by surprise and defeated. All the Israelite captives were regained and David was vindicated in the eyes of the Hebrews.

During this time Saul met a total disaster against the Philistines. The lightly armed Israelites were no match against the powerful and well-organized Philistine war-machine. The men of Israel fled from the Philistines and were killed upon the mountains of Gilboa (I Sam. 30). Saul's three sons were killed, including David's beloved friend Jonathan. Saul finally was also killed and the next day the Philistines found his body, (v. 8) stripped off the armor, and cut off his head. They sent his armor into Philistia to proclaim their victory in their temples. Finally, they put it in the house of Ashtaroth. This temple was evidently in Philistia itself and was not the temple of Ashtaroth at Beth-shan since the armor was sent back into "the land of the Philistines" proper.[147] The bodies

[147] This matter is very uncertain. Most writers seem to have overlooked the fact that the armor was sent into the "land of the Philistines." It is still possible that it was brought to Beth-shan and put in the temple there. Cf., ch. 3 on

of Saul and his three sons were fastened to the wall of Beth-shan to warn the Israelites against further rebellion.

The Philistines had found support from their "cousins," who were in control of Beth-shan and parts of the Jordan Valley, as well as from the Canaanite peoples.[148] Israel was left almost at the mercy of the Philistines who quickly resettled the captured towns. They attempted to divide the land to weaken Israelite control. Why the Philistines did not immediately pursue further subjugation of the area only the providential working of God may tell. They simply did not move quickly to finish bringing Israel under their control. Two factors may help clarify their action. First of all, the Philistines were a military aristocracy and had only a minority of people to use to resettle the Israelite territory. Secondly, Achish evidently continued to consider David his vassal after Saul's death and thus they may have thought they had all Israel under vassalage to them.

d) David's Conclusive Victory Over the Philistines (II Samuel 5)

Saul's captain, Abner, escaped the defeat at Gilboa and fled to Mahanaim of Gilead in Trans-jordan where he established Saul's son Eshbaal (or Ish-bosheth, "man of disgrace") as king of Israel. In the meantime, the elders of Judah made David their king at Hebron. However, Abner and Eshbaal were soon killed and David emerged as king over all Israel (II

"Beth-shan" for a discussion of the so-called Ashtoreth temple at Beth-shan and a picture of it as reconstructed by the excavators. For recent comments see F. James, *The Iron Age at Beth-shan* (Philadelphia: University of Pennsylvania, 1966) and H. Thompson, "Tell el-Husn–Biblical Beth-shan," *Biblical Archaeologist,* xxx (1967), pp. 110-34.

148 Cf., Wright, *BA,* xxix (1966), pp. 70-85. He shows that the various "Sea Peoples" were identified by the Hebrews by the single term "Philistines" and that they were in an alliance with the Amorites in the northern Jordan Valley. Philistine penetration of the valley went at least as far down as Tell Deir ʿAlla. The alliance with the Canaanite peoples may indicate why an Amalekite (II Sam. 1) claimed to be on the battlefield at the time of Saul's death.

Sam. 5:1).[149] David quickly moved to capture the Jebusite stronghold (later the city of David at Jerusalem) possibly by sneak attack coming up through the Jebusite water shaft (v. 8).

The Philistines then realized David's intentions and gathered in the Valley of Rephaim, south of Jerusalem, to stop him from bringing all the southern territory of Israel under his control. David's two victories over the Philistines brought final victory to Israel. He went against them in direct conflict the first time at Yahweh's instructions (v. 19) and defeated the Philistine army. The Philistines realized their strategy to cut David off from uniting with the tribes in Galilee had to work and they returned again. In the meantime, David's army had captured the religious charms of the Philistines (v. 21) and burned them in demonstration of Yahweh's victory over the artificial "gods" of the Philistines. On the second attack David's army hid behind the mulberry trees in the valley and and surprised the Philistines as the Lord went out before them to smite the Philistines (v. 24).

After the second victory David was able to chase the Philistines out of Israel never to return. He pursued them to Gezer (NEB, v. 25) and perhaps beyond. As Yahweh's *nāgîd* ("designated") and the peoples' *melek* ("king"), he was now established before all Israel as God's "anointed." The Philistines were never again able to attack Israel and the Israelites' major enemy was eliminated, allowing David to concentrate on other elements as he fully established the kingdom of Israel in the promised land, using Jerusalem as his capital.

David later brought the Philistines within the complete domain of his realm. He fortified the cities of the Shephelah for protection,[150] and then took the Philistine city of Gath

---

149 II Samuel 5:5 states that David ruled seven years as king from Hebron and thirty-three years from Jerusalem for a total of forty years.

150 Cf., Albright, *Archaeology of Palestine*, p. 122.

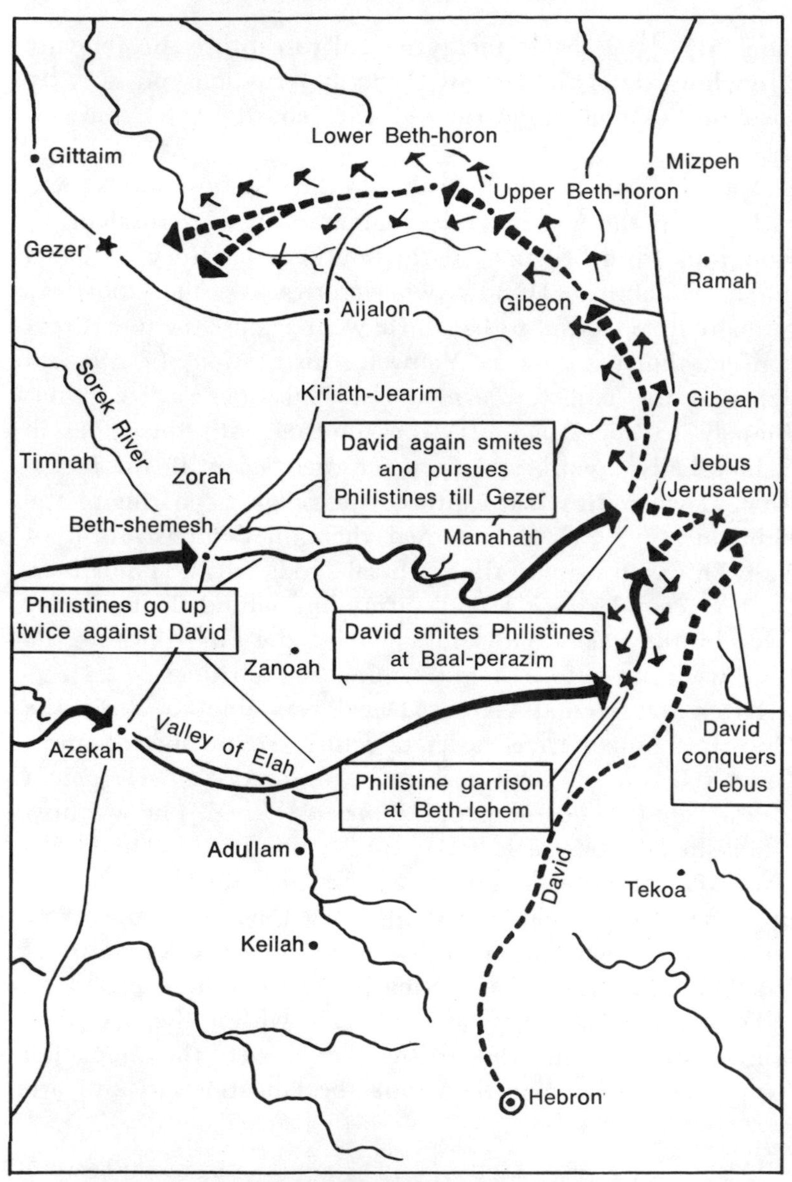

The conquest of Jebusites and Philistines

(I Chron. 18:1).[151] Gittite mercenaries became a prominent part of David's troops (II Sam. 15:18). Ultimately, he was apparently able to bring all the Philistine territory under his control as a tributary (cf. II Sam. 8:12; I Kings 4:24). More Philistine soldiers were then amalgamated with David's troops.

During the later years of the Israelite kingdom, Philistia was generally recognized as a district of its own within the territory of Israel.[152] The Philistines still appear aggressive at later times such as during the reign of Ahaz. I Kings 25:27 indicates a border conflict with the Philistines, but in general they were under tribute to Israel as in the time of Jehoshaphat (II Chron. 27:11). The latest references to the Philistines in the Old Testament appear among the books of the prophcts.

---

[151] G. E. Wright, "Fresh Evidence for the Philistine Story," *BA*, xxix (1966), p. 84, states that David recaptured all of the old Danite territory from the Philistines and this included Ekron and Gath. He left the other three major Philistine cities and Gezer somewhat independent for time because they were part of the old Egyptian grant to the Philistines. His proposal of Tell esh-Shari 'ah as Gath fits his comments very well.

[152] On later developments within Philistia see H. Tadmore, "Philistia Under Assyrian Rule," *Biblical Archaeologist,* xxix (1966), pp. 86-102. He covers the history of Philistia during the last years of Israel as well. "Philistia" appears in inscriptions of Adad-nirari, Tiglathphieser II, Sargon and Sennacherib.

Bibliography

BIBLE ATLASES

Aharoni, Y. *The Land of the Bible*. London: Burns & Oats, 1966.

Aharoni, Y. and M. Avi-Yonah, *The Macmillan Bible Atlas*. New York: Macmillan, 1968.

Grollenberg, L. *Atlas of the Bible*. New York: Nelson, 1957.

May, H. *Oxford Bible Atlas*. London: Oxford University Press, 1962.

Wright, G. E. and F. Filson, *The Westminster Historical Atlas to the Bible*. Philadelphia: Westminster, 1956.

BIBLE HISTORY

Albright, W. F. *The Biblical Period from Abraham to Ezra*. New York: Harper & Row, 1963.

——. *Yahweh and the Gods of Canaan*. Garden City, New York: Doubleday, 1969.

Barclay, W. (ed.), *The Bible and History*. Nashville and New York: Abingdon, 1968.

Beek, M. *Concise History of Israel from Abraham to the Bar Cochba Rebellion*, (trans. A. Pomerans). New York: Shocken, 1963.

Bright, J. *Early Israel in Recent History Writing*. Chicago: Allenson, 1956.

——. *A History of Israel*. Philadelphia: Westminster, 1959.

Bruce, F. F. *Israel and the Nations*. Grand Rapids, Eerdmans, 1963.

Kaufmann, Y. *The Biblical Account of the Conquest of Palestine*. Jerusalem: Magnes Press, 1953.

McKenzie, J. *The World of the Judges*. Englewood Cliffs, New Jersey: Prentice-Hall, 1966.

Merril, E. H. *An Historical Survey of the Old Testament*. Nutley, New Jersey: Craig Press, 1966.

Muilenberg, J. "The History of the Religion of Israel," in *The Interpreter's Bible*, Vol. I. New York: Abingdon, 1952, pp. 292-348.

Noth, M. *The History of Israel* (2nd ed., Eng. trans.). London: A & C Black, 1958.

——. *The Old Testament World*. Philadelphia: Fortress Press, 1966.

Oesterley, W. and T. H. Robinson, *A History of Israel*, 2 vols. Oxford: Clarendon Press, 1932.

Pedersen, J. *Israel, Its Life and Culture*, 4 vols. Copenhagen: Branner, 1926 and 1940.

Pritchard, J. B. *Ancient Near Eastern Texts*. Princeton: Princeton University Press, 1950.

Rowley, H. H. *From Joseph to Joshua* (Schweich Lectures). London: British Academy, 1950.

Schultz, S. *The Old Testament Speaks.* New York: Harper & Row, 1960.

Woudstra, M. *The Ark of the Covenant from Conquest to Kingship.* Philadelphia: Presbyterian & Reformed, 1965.

COMMENTARIES

Blaikie, W. "The First Book of Samuel," in *An Exposition of the Whole Bible,* Vol. II. Hartford: Scranton, 1908, pp. 7-112.

Bruce, F. F. "Judges," in F. Davidson (ed.), *The New Bible Commentary.* Grand Rapids: Eerdmans, 1954, pp. 236-57.

Caird, G. "The First and Second Books of Samuel," in *The Interpreter's Bible,* Vol. II. New York: Abingdon Press, 1953, pp. 855-1176.

Cassel, P. *Judges,* in J. Lange (ed.), *Commentary on the Holy Scriptures.* Grand Rapids, Zondervan, n.d. (reprint of 1871 ed.).

Crockett, W. *A Harmony of the Books of Samuel, Kings, and Chronicles.* Grand Rapids: Baker, 1951.

Cundall, A. *Judges, An Introduction and Commentary.* London: Tyndale, 1968.

Davis, J. J. *Conquest and Crisis: Studies in Joshua, Judges, and Ruth.* Grand Rapids: Baker, 1969.

Erdmann, D. *Samuel* in J. Lange (ed.), *Commentary on the Holy Scriptures.* Grand Rapids: Zondervan, n. d. (reprint of 1877 ed.).

Farrar, F. W. "Judges," in C. Ellicott (ed.), *Commentary on the Whole Bible,* Vol. II. Grand Rapids: Zondervan, n.d., pp. 170-276.

Garstang, J. *Joshua-Judges.* London: Constable & Co., 1931.

Hahn, H. *The Old Testament in Modern Research* (rev. ed.). Philadelphia: Fortress Press, 1966.

Hervey, A. *Judges* in J. Spence and J. Exell (eds.), *The Pulpit Commentary.* New York: Funk & Wagnalls, n.d.

Hyatt, J. *The Bible in Modern Scholarship.* New York: Abingdon, 1965.

Jamieson, R., A. Fausset and D. Brown, *A Commentary: Critical, Experimental, and Practical on the Old and New Testaments,* Vol. II. Grand Rapids: Eerdmans, 1945 reprint.

Keil, C. F. and F. Delitzsch, *Biblical Commentary on Joshua, Judges, and Ruth* (trans. J. Martin). Grand Rapids: Eerdmans, 1950 (reprint of 1857 ed.).

——. *Biblical Commentary on the Books of Samuel* (trans. J. Martin). Grand Rapids: Eerdmans, 1950 (reprint of 1857 ed.).

Kirkpatrick, A. F. *The First Book of Samuel* (Cambridge Bible for Schools and Colleges). Cambridge: University Press, 1880.

Lias, J. J. *The Book of Judges* (Cambridge Bible for Schools and Colleges). Cambridge University Press, 1882.

Manley, G. T. *The New Bible Handbook.* Chicago: Inter-Varsity Press, 1950.

Martin, W. J. "I Samuel," in C. F. Henry, *The Biblical Expositor.* Philadelphia: Holman, 1960.

McKenzie, J. *The World of the Judges.* Englewood Cliffs, New Jersey: Prentice Hall, 1966.

Meyers, J. M. *The Anchor Bible: I Chronicles.* Garden City, New York: Doubleday, 1965.

Meyers, J. M. and D. Elliot, "The Book of Judges," in *The Interpreter's Bible,* Vol. II. New York: Abingdon, 1953, pp. 677-828.

Moore, G. F. *A Critical and Exegetical Commentary on Judges* (International Critical Commentary). New York: Scribner's Sons, 1909.
Renwick, A. M. "I and II Samuel," in F. Davidson (ed.), *The New Bible Commentary*. Grand Rapids: Eerdmans, 1954, pp. 262-99.
Rigg, W. H. *The First Book of Samuel*. London: Religious Tract Society, n.d.
Rowley, H. H. (ed.), *The Old Testament and Modern Study*. Oxford: Clarendon Press, 1961.
Smith, H. P. *A Critical and Exegetical Commentary on the Books of Samuel* (International Critical Commentary). New York: Scribner's Sons, 1909.
Smith, R. "I Samuel" in H. Spence and J. Exell (eds.), *The Pulpit Commentary*. New York: Funk and Wagnalls, n.d.
Spence, H. "I Samuel," in C. Ellicott (ed.), *Commentary on the Whole Bible*, Vol. II. Grand Rapids: Zondervan, n.d.
Terry, M. S. "Book of Judges to II Samuel," in *Commentary on the Old Testament*, Vol. III. New York: Nelson & Phillips, 1875, pp. 151-558.
Watson, R. "The Book of Judges," in *An Exposition of the Bible*, Vol. I. Hartford: Scranton, 1908, pp. 743-833.
——. "Judges and Ruth," in R. Nicoll (ed.), *The Expositor's Bible*. New York: Funk and Wagnalls, 1900, pp. 3-420.
Wilson, C. R. "Judges" and "I Samuel" in *The Wesleyan Bible Commentary*, Vol. II. Grand Rapids: Eerdmans, 1967, pp. 59-116; 133-232.
Young, F. "Judges," in C. F. Henry (ed.), *The Biblical Expositor*. Philadelphia: Holman, 1960.
Young, R. *Analytical Concordance to the Bible*. Grand Rapids: Eerdmans, n.d.

ARCHAEOLOGY

Books:

Abramsky, S. *Ancient Towns in Israel*. Jerusalem: World Zionist Organization, 1963.
Adams, J. M. *Ancient Records and the Bible*. Nashville: Broadman, 1946.
Albright, W. F. *Archaeology and the Religion of Israel* (Ayer Lectures). Baltimore: John Hopkins Press, 1942.
——. *From Stone Age to Christianity*. Garden City, New York: Doubleday. 1957.
——. *Recent Discoveries in Bible Lands*. New York: Funk & Wagnalls, n.d. (included as a supplement to "Young's Analytical Concordance").
——. *The Archaeology of Palestine*. Baltimore: Penguin Books, 1960.
——. *The Biblical Period from Abraham to Ezra*. New York: Harper & Row, 1963.
Bliss, F. and R. A. S. Macalister, *Excavations in Palestine During the Years 1898-1900*. London: Palestine Exploration Fund, 1902.
Boudet, J. *Jerusalem: a History*. New York: Putnam's Sons, 1967.
Childe, V. G. *New Light on the Most Ancient East*. New York: Grove Press, 1957.
Dothan, M. & D. N. Freedman, *Ashdod, the First Season of Excavations*. Jerusalem: Atiqot, 1967 (English series).
Ehrich, R. *Relative Chronologies in Old World Archaeology*. Chicago: University of Chicago Press, 1954.
Epstein, C. *Palestinian Bichrome Ware*. Leiden: Brill, 1966.

Finegan, J. *Light from the Ancient Past.* Princeton: Princeton University Press, 1959.

Franken, H. J. *Excavations at Tell Deir ʿAllā*. Leiden: Brill, 1969.

Gordon, C. H. *Introduction to Old Testament Times.* Ventor, New Jersey: Ventor Press, 1953.

Glueck, N. *Rivers in the Desert.* New York: Farrar, Strauss & Cudahy, 1959.

——. *The River Jordan.* New York: McGraw-Hill, 1968.

Grant, E. *Beth-shemesh,* Haverford, Pennsylvania: Haverford Archaeological Expedition, 1929.

Gray, J. *The Canaanites.* New York: Praeger, 1964.

James, F. *The Iron Age at Beth-shan.* Philadelphia: University of Pennsylvania, 1966.

Kelso, J. *Archaeology and the Ancient Testament.* Grand Rapids: Zondervan, 1968.

Kenyon, F. *The Bible and Archaeology.* London: Marshall, Morgan, Scott, 1940.

Kenyon, K. *Archaeology in the Holy Land.* New York: Praeger, 1966.

Kitchen, K. A. *Ancient Orient and Old Testament.* Chicago: Inter-Varsity Press, 1966.

Macalister, R.A.S. *The Philistines: Their History and Civilization* (Schweich Lectures). London: British Academy, 1913.

——. *The Excavation of Gezer,* 3 vols. London: Murray, 1912.

——. *A Century of Excavation in Palestine.* New York: Revell, 1925.

Mallon, A. *Teleilāt Ghassūl,* 2 vols. Rome: Pontifical Biblical Institute, 1934.

McClintock, J. and J. Strong, *Cyclopedia of Biblical, Theological, and Ecclesiastical Literature* Vol. VIII. New York: Harper & Brothers, 1891. Reprint. Grand Rapids: Baker Book House, 1970.

McCown, C. *Tell En-Naṣbeh,* 2 vols. New Haven: American Schools of Oriental Research, 1947.

Meyer, M. A. *History of the City of Gaza.* New York: Columbia University Press, 1907.

Mitchell, T. C. "Philistia," in D. W. Thomas (ed.), *Archaeology and Old Testament Study.* Oxford: Clarendon Press, 1967.

Moscati, S. *Ancient Semitic Civilization.* London: Elek Books, 1957.

Noordtzij, A. *De Filistijnen.* Kempen: Kok, 1905.

Pearlman, M. and Y. Yannai, *Historical Sites in Israel.* London: Alden, 1964.

Petrie, F. Tell el-Ḥesi. London: British School of Archacology in Egypt, 1891.

——. *Gerar.* London: British School of Archaeology in Egypt, 1928.

——. *Beth-pelet* (Tell Fara), 2 vols. London: British School of Archaeology in Egypt, 1930-32.

——. *Ancient Gaza,* 4 vols. London: British School of Archaeology in Egypt, 1931-34.

Pritchard, J. B. *Palestinian Figurines in Relation to Certain Goddesses Known Through Literature.* Philadelphia: University of Pennsylvania, 1943.

Rowe, A. *Beth-shan:History and Topography.* Philadelphia: University of Pennsylvania, 1930.

——. *Beth-shan: The Four Canaanite Temples.* Philadelphia: University of Pennsylvania, 1940.

Thomas, D. W. *Documents From Old Testament Times.* New York: Harper & Row, 1965.

Thompson, J. *Archaeology and the Old Testament.* Grand Rapids: Eerdmans, 1957.

Tufnell, O. *Lachish,* Vol. III & IV. London: Oxford University Press, 1953, 1958.
Unger, M. *Archaeology and the Old Testament.* Grand Rapids: Zondervan, 1954.
Watzinger, C. *Tell el-Mutesellim.* Leipzig: Hinrichs'sche Buchhandlung, 1929.
Wright, G. E. *Biblical Archaeology.* Philadelphia: Westminster, 1960.
Wright, G. E. (ed.), *The Bible and the Ancient Near East* (Essays in honor of W. F. Albright). Garden City: Doubleday, 1965.
Yadin, Y., Y. Aharoni, et. al. *Hazor I* and *Hazor II.* Jerusalem: Magnes Press, 1958.

Articles:

Aharoni, Y. "Forerunners of the Limes: Iron Age Fortresses in the Negev," *Israel Exploration Journal,* pp. 1-17.
Albright, W. F. "The Sea Peoples in Palestine," *The Cambridge Ancient History.* Cambridge: Clarendon Press, 1966; ii, ch. xxxiii, pp. 24-33.
——. "The Chronology of a South Palestinian City, Tell el-'Ajjûl," *American Journal of Semitic Languages and Literatures,* iv (1938), pp. 337-59.
Astour, M. "The Origin of the Terms 'Canaan,' 'Phoenician,' and 'Purple,'" *Journal of Near Eastern Studies,* xxiv (1965), pp. 346-50.
Barag, D. "A Survey of Pottery Rescued from the Sea off the Coast of Israel," *Israel Exploration Journal,* xiii (1963), pp. 13-19.
Benson, J. "A Problem in Orientalizing Cretan Birds," *Journal of Near Eastern Studies,* xx (1961), pp. 73-84 (includes pictures).
Berard, J. "*Philistins et Prèκξ‾ξnés,*" *Revue Archaeologique,* xxxvii (1951), pp. 129-42.
Bonfante, G. "Who Were the Philistines?" American Journal of Archaeology, 50 (1946), pp. 251-62.
Bulow, R. and R. Mitchell, "Report of the Excavations at Tell en-Nagila," *Israel Exploration Journal,* xi (1961), pp. 101-10.
Campbell, E. "In Search of the Philistines," *Biblical Archaeologist,* xxvi (1963), pp. 30-32.
Condor, C. "Philistincs," *International Standard Bible Encyclopedia,* Vol. IV. Chicago: Howard-Severance, 1915; pp. 2376-83.
Cross, F. "The Tabernacle," *Biblical Archaeologist,* x (1947), pp. 45-68.
Cross, F. and D. N. Freedman, "The Name of Ashdod," *Bulletin of the American Schools of Oriental Research,* 175 (1964), pp. 48-50.
Delcor, M. "*Jahweh et Dagon; ou le Jahwisme face à la religion des Philistins, d'après* I Sam. V." *Vetus Testamentum,* 14 (1964), pp. 136-54.
Dever, W. "Excavations at Gezer," *Biblical Archaeologist,* xxx (1967), pp. 47-62.
Diringer, D. "The Royal Jar-Handle Stamps of Ancient Judah," *Biblical Archaeologist,* xii (1949), pp. 70-85.
Dothan, M. "Ashdod," *Revue Biblique,* 74 (1967), pp. 78-80.
——. "Revealing the Past of Ancient Ashdod," *Illustrated London News,* 6487 (1963), pp. 904-906; 944-46 (20 figures).
Dothan, T. "Archaeological Reflections on the Philistine Problem," *Antiquity & Survival,* ii (1957), pp. 151-64.
Eissfeldt, O. "*Philister,*" *Paulys Real-Encyclopedia,* xxxviii (1938), pp. 2390-401.
Freedman, D. N. "The Second Season at Ancient Ashdod," *Biblical Archaeologist,* xxvi (1963), pp. 134-39.
Furumark, A. "Philistine Ware," in *The Chronology of Mycenaean Pottery.* Chicago: University of Chicago Press, 1941; pp. 118-21.

Garstang, J. "Excavations at Ashkelon," *Palestine Exploration Quarterly,* lii (1920), p. 156.

Gordon, C. H. "The Role of the Philistines," *Antiquity,* xxx (1956), pp. 22-26.

Grant, E. "The Philistines," *Journal of Biblical Literature,* lv (1936), pp. 175-94.

Graybill, J. "Philistines," in M. Tenney (ed.), *Zondervan Pictorial Bible Dictionary.* Grand Rapids: Zondervan, 1963; pp. 651-52.

Hankey, V. "Late Mycenaean Pottery at Beth-shan," *American Journal of Archaeology,* lxx (1966), pp. 169-71.

Heurtley, W. "The Relationship Between 'Philistine' and Mycenaean Pottery," *Quarterly of the Department of Antiquities in Palestine,* v (1936), pp. 90-110.

Hoffer, H. "A Hittite Analog to the David and Goliath Contest of Champions," *Catholic Biblical Quarterly,* xxx (1968), pp. 651-52.

Kaplan, J. "*Yavneh-Yam et Ashdod-yam,*" *Revue Biblique,* 75 (1968), pp. 402-404.

Kassis, H. "Gath and the Structure of the Philistine Society," *Journal of Biblical Literature,* 84 (1965), pp. 259-71.

Kitchen, K. "Aegean Place Name in a List of Amenophis III," *Bulletin of the American Schools of Oriental Research,* 181 (1966), pp. 23-24.

Lance, H. "Gezer in the Land and in History," *Biblical Archaeologist,* xxiv (1961), pp. 66-85.

Lapp, P. "Tell el-Fûl," *Biblical Archaeologist,* xxviii (1965), pp. 2-9.

MacKenzie, D. "Excavations at Ain Shems," *Palestine Exploration Fund* Annual, i (1911), pp. 41-94.

MacLaurin, E. "Anak/'Avae," *Vetus Testamentum,* xv (1965), pp. 468-74.

Maisler, B. "The Stratification of Tell Abū Hawâm on the Bay of Acre," *Bulletin of the American Schools of Oriental Research,* 124 (1951), pp. 21-25.

Mazor, B. "The Philistines and the Rise of Israel and Tyre," *Proceedings of the Israel Academy of Sciences and Humanities,* I (1964), p. 7.

Mendelsohn, I. "Samuel's Denunciation of Kingship in Light of the Akkadian Documents from Ugarit," *Bulletin of the American Schools of Oriental Research,* 143 (1956), pp. 17-21.

Mendenhall, G. "The Hebrew Conquest of Palestine," *Biblical Archaeologist,* xxv (1962), pp. 66-85.

Milik, J. "An Unpublished Arrow-Head with Phonecian Inscription of the 11th-10th Century B.C.," *Bulletin of the American Schools of Oriental Research,* 143 (1956), pp. 3-5.

Milik, J. and F. M. Cross, "Inscribed Javelin-heads from the Period of the Judges," *Bulletin of the American Schools of Oriental Research,* 134 (1954), pp. 5-14.

Millard, A. R. "A Letter from the Ruler of Gezer," *Palestine Exploration Quarterly,* 100 (1965), pp. 140-43.

Mitchell, T. C. "Philistines," in J. Douglas (ed.), *New Bible Dictionary.* Grand Rapids: Eerdmans, 1962, pp. 988-91.

Navah, J. "Khirbat al-Muqanna': Ekron," *Israel Exploration Journal,* viii (1958), pp. 87-100.

Patai, R. "The Godess Asherah," *Journal of Near Eastern Studies,* xxiv (1965), pp. 37-52.

Phythian-Adams, W. "Philistine Origins," *Palestine Exploration Quarterly,* lv (1923), pp. 11-36.

Rahtjen, B. "Philistine and Hebrew Amphictyonies," *Journal of Near Eastern Studies,* xxiv (1965), pp. 100-104.

Rainey, A. F. "The Kingdom of Ugarit," *Biblical Archaeologist,* xxviii (1965), pp. 134-39.

Ross, J. "Gezer in the Tell el-Amarna Letters," *Biblical Archaeologist,* xxx (1967), pp. 62-70.

Scott, R. B. Y. "The Shekel Sign on Stone Weights," *Bulletin of the American Schools of Oriental Research,* 153 (1959), pp. 32-34.

——. "Shekel-fraction Markings on Hebrew Weights," *Bulletin of the American Schools of Oriental Research,* 173 (1964), pp. 53-63.

Seebas, H. "I Sam. 15 *als Schlüssel für das Verständnis der Sogenannten Königs freund lichen Reihe* I Sam. 9:1-10:16," *Zeitschrift fur die alttestament liche Wissenschaft,* 78 (1966), pp. 148-79.

Seger, J. "Why We Dig at Gezer," *Hartford Quarterly,* vii (1967), pp. 19-39.

Sukenik, E. "Excavations in Palestine, 1933-4," *Palestine Department of Antiquities Quarterly,* iv (1935), p. 208 f., 225.

Tadmor, H. "Philistia Under Assyrian Rule," *Biblical Archaeologist,* xxix (1966), pp. 86-102.

Thompson, H. "Tell el-Husn: Biblical Beth-shan," *Biblical Archaeologist,* xxx (1967), pp. 110-35.

Van Beek, G. "Cypriot Chronology and the Dating of Iron I Sites in Palestine," *Bulletin of the American Schools of Oriental Research,* 124 (1951), pp. 26-28.

van Selms, A. "Judge Shamgar (Judges 3:31)," *Vetus Testamentum,* xiv (1964), pp. 294-309.

van Uchelen, N. "*De Filistijnen in Let Oude Testament; beeld en Werkelijkheid,*" *Netherlands Theologisch Tijdschrift,* xx (1966), pp. 339-53.

Waldbaum, J. "Philistine Tombs at Tell Fara and their Aegean Prototypes," *American Journal of Archaeology,* lxx (1966), pp. 331-40.

Warren, R. "Approximate Latitudes, Longitudes and Altitudes Above Mean Sea Level of Points in the Plain of Philistia," *Palestine Exploration Fund Quarterly Statement,* ii (1871), pp. 162-64.

Weiser, A. "*Samuels Philister-Sieg; die Uberlieferungen in* I Samuel VII," *Zeitschriftfür Theologie und Kirche,* lvi (1959), pp. 253-72.

Wright, G. E. "The Discoveries at Megiddo, 1935-39," *Biblical Archaeologist,* xiii (1950), pp. 23-45.

——. "Philistine Coffins and Mercenaries," *Biblical Archaeologist,* xxii (1959), pp. 54-66.

——. "Fresh Evidence for the Philistine Story," *Biblical Archaeologist,* xxix (1966), pp. 70-86.

——. "Israelite Samaria and Iron Age Chronology," *Bulletin of the American Schools of Oriental Research,* 155 (1959), pp. 13-28.

——. "Gezer" *Revue Biblique,* 74 (1967), pp. 72-73.

Yeiven, S. "Tell Gath," *Israel Exploration Journal,* vi (1956), p. 258 j.; vii (1957), p. 264 j.; viii (1958), p. 274-76; ix (1959), pp. 269-71; x (1960), p. 122 f.

——. "Early Contacts Between Canaan and Egypt," *Israel Exploration Journal,* x (1960), pp. 193-203.

Index